Con

Character References

My grandparents inspire people all over the world every day. Growing up they have taught me that God love us unconditionally. I have taken this with me throughout my life. With all the Love in the world, your oldest granddaughter Heather Perilloux

Richard and Linda Cosentino are to me, a prototype of Christ DNA centered couples. Their dedication and commitment to each other spills over into their written words. This couple has deeply impressed me with the depth and breadth of their research. Their quest for Spirit Truth is clearly the motivation force of their life. I am convinced that these daily insights for Personal Spiritual Truth, will speak uplifting and motivational light into every seeker of a more fulfilling life. Respectfully submitted, Rudy Jones

Richard and Linda Cosentino, who are not just our best friends but our mentors. Thank you for an amazing journey and introducing us to our God Parents, Mother and Father God. After reading this book we are convinced that your readers will know, they have an invitation to meet God and they have arrived home. Love Bruce and Debra Lapierre.

Over forty years ago, Linda and Richard and their three children walked into a Sunday service and I happen to turn around and knew immediately we would become close friends, and that we did. Linda, was back when, was receiving some deep truths of God, and as she shared them with me I would just glean from her. Linda has dedicated her entire life to seeking the deeper things of god and he has entrusted these truths with her. I will always remain grateful to her and a true friend in Christ. Forever love, Arleen Brignac

Linda Cosentino has devoted her life to bringing the Light of Sprit into other's lives. Her lessons are always Sprit led. She is a great source of inspiration on a daily basis. Love Jo Hanna

Linda is good friend, you seldom find in a lifetime. Love Martha Ruhter

About the Author

Linda Cosentino has been married for 56 years. This says a lot about living this life at a higher peaceful level in the sprit realm. Linda has an email list of lessons each day about God. Linda has studied these bible principals for 45 years and continues each day studying the deep things of God. Linda has taught many classes in her 45 years of study. Linda has a website with back lessons written each day. The website is www.thegodinus.com

HAPPY NEW YEAR

January

January 1-WE WANT TO HAVE PEACE ON EARTH -
This is a New Year, New Beginnings, New Thoughts,
Healthy Bodies, Minds cleansed of negative thoughts, new
opportunities. My mind is transformed to the Mind of God.
I clean the windows of my mind to be clear and clean of all
negative thoughts that hinder my plan and purpose.
Ephesians 4:24- "Put on the new man that God is created in
righteousness and true holiness." The song that says,
"Hark the herald (messenger, announce, foretell) Angels
sing, Glory be to the New Born King, Peace on earth and
mercy mild, God and sinners reconcile (bring back to our
original state)."

January 2-EACH DAY MY INSPIRATION COMES
FROM GOD. I can put on the Mind of Christ. God is in
control of my every thought, every act, every breath, every
place I walk with Love, Peace, and Joy. I have the key to
open my doorway of my mind to everything that is positive
instead of negative thoughts. I can walk in a higher
dimension where God's presence is always there bringing
Light, Understanding, Love, Peace and Joy. I listen to the
Still Small Voice within me that directs me what to do.

1

January 3-PRUNING MEANS CUTTING AWAY OF BRANCHES THAT ARE NEGATIVE THOUGHTS THAT ARE NOT HEALTHY. Pruning is necessary to make my Life beautiful in order for the negative thoughts to be cut off with thoughts of God to take its place. All my doubts, fears, unhappiness, unpleasant things that happen let me not dwell on it, and let it go so I can receive the best of my being today. All fear thoughts of worry, doubt etc. that crowds my mind with negative thoughts and feelings must be Let Go. I must know that everything is going to be ALRIGHT. God is in control of my life.

January 4-WHY IS THIS HAPPENING, GOD? No one can rob us, but our own thoughts that we create. When Jesus was on the cross He did not say, "My God, My God why have thy forsaken me?" He said, "God you will never forsake me." God cannot enter in a war, strife or a pig pen. The Prodigal son said "How many hired servants of my Father's house have bread enough, and to spare, and I perish with hunger?" Things go wrong because God of your being is not Being God. We need to change our thinking and know that God is within us. The only one problem is the belief that we are separated from God.

January 5-WE CAN HAVE A CHANGED LIFE. When we real-eyes Christ AS the center of our Being, we are changed. Name means the nature of your Being. Saul changed his name to Paul (made small; restrained). Jacob means supplanted, father of lies name was changed to Israel Prince with God. I used to criticize myself and say, "I AM not smart enough, pretty enough and the list went on and on. One Day a Voice came into my mind saying, "Why do you constantly criticize my Perfect Creation? This is when I real-eyes that the Christ was the center of my Being.

January 6-THE CHRIST IS WASHING OUR FEET. The feet are the symbol of strength stability. We need our feet to support the rest of the body. Cleansing of the feet from the dirt (lowest of human thinking) is necessary to clear away all thoughts of the human body. "Every place that the sole of your foot shall tread upon, to you have I given it, as I spoke unto Moses." The feet go all day directed by the Mind of Christ or the Mind of the carnal nature that has no reality. The shoes (manmade) pick up the negative influence of world and that is why the feet have to be cleansed. Feet Washing is an allegory. We do not have to go around washing each other's feet.

January 7-I SPEAK ONLY GODLY WORDS. I speak the word of Love and the Love of God surrounds me, and I can feel THE PRESENCE When I AM upset about anything, I can change my thoughts to the thoughts of peace. I AM Love because God is Love. I speak Health and healing to my body, knowing that My Father brings to me wholeness into my Being. Lead me to a person that I can share what God is teaching me. I speak Happiness to all my family no matter what is in their lives at the moment. I speak that everything in me reflects the Christ in me in everything I say and do. "Thou shall declare a thing, and it shall be established unto thee." Job 22:28

January 8- What is MEANING OF THE CUP? A cup is used to drink out of. John 18:11-"The cup which the Father has given me, shall I not drink it?" To drink of a cup means to take in faith, "Seeing the substance hoped for manifested." Drinking of the Living Water is done by dying out to self and becoming alive to Christ, and my having a new spiritual life. We can change lemons to lemonade. "A spoonful of sugar makes the medicine go down." Sword is for fighting, but you can put thoughts or the sword back into the sheath and think thoughts of peace.

January 9-WHAT HAVE YOU BEEN TAUGHT? The terrorist have been taught to kill the infidel (one who rejects a religion that is all of us). Paul thought he was doing God a service by persecuting (torment continuously for one's belief) the Christians. We are taught that God is waiting for us to step out of line so He can punish us. We were not taught that God is Unconditional Love. We are not taught that at the cross Jesus took away all sin, (missing the mark of Being God like), sickness, and gave us eternal life. We are not taught that we are created in the image (reflection in a mirror) and likeness (exact copy) of God both male and female. If we knew that God dwelled in each one of us, we would stop judgment and criticizing every one and see them as God's children of royalty instead of human beings.

January 10-I CAN HAVE A MIND OF THOUGHTS THAT ARE POSITIVE. When things go good, we know that God is in control. In a time of troubles, we have a thought that "Where is God?" Sometimes we think that God has forgotten us. I know that every situation in my life is to teach me Unconditional Love and know that everything will be OK. The thought occurs of what could possibly be good in this situation. God always means it for good. "I live and move and have my being in God." I open up my consciousness to receive only the best for my life, and knowing God's perfect action is in my life teaching me what I have to change in my thoughts to the thoughts of God.

January 11 -WALLS ARE FALLING DOWN IN MY LIFE NOW. Joshua 6:5-"All the people shout with a great shout; and the walls of the city (we are the city of God) shall fall down flat." Walls are anything in life that is negative that is not the best for us and prevents us from experiencing life in the fullest and restricts us from Being God like in everything we do and say. Fear (false evidence appearing real) is the main barrier that we feel in any situation that seems to be a threat. "Perfect Love cast out fear." "I AM." I know that everything is going to be alright.

January 12-I AM SEEING THINGS AS THEY ARE. A diamond is cut and polished with many facets. We are all a diamond in the rough. Diamonds are a sign of Unconditional Love. A pearl needs much sandpaper of other people to make it smooth and round. The human body has many parts but is still One Body and every part has a special function. There are many mansions (dwelling places for God to dwell in that is unique). The word Christ means anointed ones. We are the Christ of God. Peter said, "Jesus is the Christ, the Son of the Living God." "We are heirs of God and joint heirs with Jesus the Christ." God is in each of us making us God Beings or the children of God. God created man in his image.

January 13-HOW DID JESUS THE CHRIST HEAL? He did not see the person with pain, suffering, and so on. He saw us as God created us. He went into the realm of Spirit where there is no pain or suffering. He conveyed to their minds that they were whole and complete. We believe that God sees us healed. This healing power is working in my body as I write. I know it is not I, but the Christ in my Being. In the realm of Spirit, only positive thoughts can exist. . There is no EGO thinking that edges God out. I receive healing in every cell of my body and all cells are very healthy. I have no fear or doubt that everything is healed.

January 14-GOD'S POWER IN CONTROL OF ME HEALS ME. "Thou will keep him in perfect peace whose mind is stayed on thee; because he trusted in thee." Is. 26:3. There is an active Presence that is moving in everything we do and say at the very center of our Being. This presence is in every cell, every organ, and every function of my body. This Power is working in my body right now, and no illness can withstand it. God is in my life, and I cannot be sick. Where ever I have a problem, the healing Truth will cause the problem to dissolve and set me free. My thoughts are only Happy, Joyful, full of God's Love and chosen Peace that is beyond understanding. I can TURN ON THE LIGHT and darkness will disappear.

January 15-THE SPEAKING TONGUE HAS POWER. The tongue is a powerful organ. It can be an agent of the Spirit by giving the Truth to others. Can you remember someone saying something cruel to you as a child, and you often think of what they said so long ago to affect the present of you now? The tongue is one of the five senses of taste. Let us taste the sweet realm of the Spirit with all the Love, Peace, and Happiness. A gentle word to another person can change their lives even for a moment. "Power of Life and Death is in the tongue." Compliments to another person can change their face to a smile and let them stop thinking about their problems. They will say, "You made my day." I want to speak only God's words.

January-16 THE NOZZLE IN OUR MIND. A nozzle at the end of a water hose can only produce the water supplied to it. Let us look at the water as thoughts flowing from our mind. Our mind is conditioned to this world, perhaps even thoughts from ancestors thru DNA or even from previous lives if that is our belief. This is why we must daily train our mind at a higher SPIRITUAL level. The more we accomplish this we will see our thoughts transformed from suspicion, anger and fear to water that gently nourishes the earth before us. Then our path becomes peaceful and our way more assured.

January 17-TRAFFIC RULES HAVE A PURPOSE. Do you get angry when driving when someone runs in front of you or cuts you off and you have to make a quick stop in order not to get into an accident? First of all, anger is never God. Being negative leads us to body aches and pains and does not help our health condition. Forgiveness is not only for us, but for the other person also to completely erase all hurts on both sides. When another driver is doing something you don't approve of, forgive them and then the forgiveness goes out to the world and the other driver stops driving ridicules. Does it seem impossible to change someone thoughts in another car? Remember thoughts are creative.

7

January 18- HUMPTY DUMPTY HAD A GREAT FALL.
This lesson is about us. "Humpty Dumpy sat on a wall."
A wall represents all the past and future thoughts that stop
us from receiving Present Spiritual truth. A wall that
separates us from Being One with each other. "All of the
king's horses and all the king's men could not put Humpty
Dumpy back together again." All the king's horses are the
power and the king's men are the thoughts that **E**dge **G**od
Out The real King is God. The real King's men know the
Truths of God. They can fix Humpty Dumpty, the egg that
should grow to Spiritual maturity, providing us with
Spiritual food to bring our body to resurrection Life.

January 19- DREAMS THAT ARE NOT NICE GIVES US
FEAR. "Fear is false evidence appearing real. "Perfect
Love cast out fear." Before you go to bed, ask God to bless
your dreams. Nip the disturbing dreams in the bud and
know that they cannot hurt you. The effect of our thoughts
is how we relate to the situation. God's peace is yours.
"Whatever is true, worthy, just, pure; lovely and loveable,
kind, and gracious, fix your minds on them." We can
choose to experience peace, health abundance and success.
Darkness (negative thinking) does not exist only in our own
thoughts. Bad dreams are the same in that they are not real.

January 20-WE CAN'T BE CONCERNED FROM APPEARANCES OF LACK. "We Let Go and Let God." We have the Power of God on our side within us at all times. I have the strength to do all that needs to be done Be like the little engine that brought presents to the children from our book "Fairy Tales Can Come True page 22. The Little engine said, "I THINK I CAN." Other engines representing the ego thoughts that Edge God Out said, you are too small not powerful enough, not pretty enough and so on. This is the ego thoughts that are a liar and a deceiver. Let us choose peace instead of Being Right and Swallow pride to save an argument. See beauty in people instead of faults.

January 21-I CAN SEE DIFFERENTLY. A person changes from being angry to experiencing joy when you give them a compliment. The past is gone and can be erased with its negative energy. We only live NOW in the present. If you see strife in your life, you can change the channel and see peace instead. Shake off anger. A Spirit Being cannot have sickness, pain, strife, death and unhappiness. Can we visualize a person perfect, filled with Light permeating every cell of their body? We are the very Christ the sons and daughters of the Living God.

January 22-SERPENT LIFTED UP. "The serpent was more subtle (crafty; not obvious) than all the other thoughts." This is the thoughts of the ego that EDGES GOD OUT. The serpent represents the lowest of human thoughts and crawls on its belly in the dirt. When Moses lifted up the human thoughts of the serpent to the Spiritual realm, they were healed. When we turn our thoughts to the Spirit within, the whole man is lifted up to the Christ, the sons and daughters of the Living God. "If I be lifted up from the earth (human thoughts) will draw unto me." I AM HEALED.

9

January 23-THE EARTH IS FILLED WITH THE GLORY OF GOD. This means we are the earth that is filled with the glory of God. The Spirit Beings gathered together and said, "What if there was something instead of God?" Then the fallen thoughts came into a lower dimension to the world of duality believing in good and evil. Jesus the Christ gave us one thought, "Love God and Love your neighbor as yourself." We are to see every one perfect as God created them. The Christ in me writes my lessons. There is nothing that is by accident or by chance.

January 24-PRECIOUS MOMENTS THAT BRINGS US HAPPINESS. "Precious Moments could be like a fragrant bottle that we can splash it on every day?" The negative things in the past would be completely erased from your memory. It is a present from God wrapped in gold paper. The present can be filled with Love, Peace, and Joy. When we pass by a person, they will know who and what they are by the smell of this perfume. They will want to have the same things happen to them as well. The whole world will be filled NOT with human thinking, beliefs, control of others, but the thoughts of God.

January 25-SEEDS HAVE MEANINGS. A new plant grows from the seed planted. Matt. 13:37-"He who sows the good seed is the SON OF MAN." 1 Peter 1:23-"You have been regenerated-born again-not of mortal origin, but immortal by the ever living WORD OF GOD." "Whatever you sow, you shall reap." A caterpillar eats the dirt of human thoughts. The cocoon progression takes only the truth of what is eaten and leaves the religious teachings and beliefs behind. The beautiful butterfly emerges and eats only the sweet nectar of the Spirit realm. The butterfly represents resurrection of human thoughts to the thoughts of God.

January 26-LEAVES HAVE SPIRITUAL MEANINGS. I AM going to compare the leaves with our lives. Autumn is when the leaves appear as different beautiful colors. Red for Love, Yellow for the Christ which is the sons and daughters of God, happiness, positive, Brown is for dependability, Green-meaning life and harmony, and they are all blended together to perform a beautiful arrangement of colors. The fallen leaves represent all the negative things in our lives which must fall off the tree in order to become God like in our Being. In the winter everything seems to be dead and fallen asleep. We can die to religious teachings, beliefs that humans have taught us. Spring comes from a cold winter and we look up at the barren trees with new leaves on them. We are awaken and resurrecting from death to Life with all the green everywhere.

January 27-WE CAN HAVE A SECOND TOUCH FROM GOD. There was a man that was blind from birth. Jesus the Christ took some clay (lowest of human thinking) and put it in his eyes. Jesus the Christ touched the man the second time and this time the man saw very clearly. Simon helped Jesus to carry the cross to the finish line. Mary came to visit her cousin and the baby leaped in her. Whatever is bothering you now, "This too shall pass and the second touch will be waiting for you to receive.

January 28-I AM AWAKENING FROM THE DREAM. We are in a dream state of thinking that this world is a physical world instead of a Spiritual World. We are dreaming we are sick, suffering, having all kinds of pain and disease. Belief in two powers is real in the dream. The Christ came to awaken us from this dream state to see God only. Fear, sickness, hurricanes, or any negative thinking has no power. The Christ came to teach us the God of Unconditional Love. We are Spirit Beings instead of human beings. Everything and everyone is a Spiritual creation spoken into existence by God. We are the words that shall never pass away. God is the only Power.

January 29-GOD IS ALL THERE IS. You are created in the Image (reflection in a mirror) and Likeness (exact copy) of God both male and female. We are the children of God. If we think we are God, we fall into the ego thinking that Edges God Out and duped into believing a lie. We do not live in a physical body or universe. We are an individual expression of the Living God. Sickness, pain, suffering can only be a lie and waiting for me to awaken from this dream state that is not God. The Kingdom of God is within you and me. How can I have any negative thought when God is ALL THERE IS? So I must stop trying to do everything by my own human thoughts. My thoughts must be transformed to God's thoughts.

January 30-APRIL SHOWERS BRINGS THE MAY
FLOWERS. Shower is a brief fall of rain; party with gifts
for the bride. "Behold, I create a new heaven (Spirit realm)
and a new earth and the former shall not be remembered,
nor comes into mind." How refreshing is the air after a
rain. I can empty my mind of past thoughts of fear, doubt,
condemnation and so forth when the dew of the morning
comes with the dawn of this new day. I can choose to
refresh my mind with showers of Truth that sets me free
from old human beliefs and man- made laws. We can
receive showers of blessings and know who and what we
are.

January 31-GOD IS ACCELERATING MY GROWTH.
Every day is a process to re-member and to receive what
God is revealing to you and me. We plant a seed which is
the beginning of a process. If we are impatient and dig the
seed up, it will never become what it was meant to be. We
know that "I" of my own self can't do the work but the
Christ in me that does the animation of the body. We are
Spirit because everything God creates is Spiritual. We are
not God. We are the temple of the Living God that God
dwells in you and in me. This is the time of great Spiritual
advancement and awaking.
Countless seeds have been planted through the ages, could
this be the time of our spiritual completion? This is the time
we see God as He really is and be Like Him.

February

February 1-LET US MOVE FORWARD. The past is dead events that will never be in the present again unless we bring them up. We only live in the NOW with no past and no future. Today is peace, joy and happiness. We must let the past go and let God rule our Now's. Love your enemies, do good to them which hate you, bless them that curse you and pray for those who despitefully use you?" This statement in the natural carnal mind is impossible. If you want to be in the Spirit realm and BE God like, we must see them differently. God dwells in them. The Now says, "EVERY THING IS GOING TO BE ALRIGHT." "This, too, shall pass."

February 2-LET US OVERTURN THE MONEY CHANGES. The money changes are nothing to do with money. It has everything to do what needs to be deleted within your own life. Re-member the money changes are in the temple (mind) of our Being. Let us overturn sin to not missing the mark of Being, sickness to health, Life to death, jealousy to happiness for someone's progress; envy to knowing you have it all, poverty to wealth, guilt to knowing no guilt but forgiveness, hate to love because Love is all there is. There is only one Mind, the Mind of Christ, and One Power. Good and evil does not exist in God. God is in us and we know that it is not "I" but the Christ in me.

February 3-THIS IS THE SPIRITUAL TRUTHS ABOUT THE 10 COMMANDMENTS. No power given to good or evil and making a man a god because of the teachings. Images are what we have in our minds about sin, sickness, death pain and suffering. No curse words to describe our emotions. All days are God's Days. We are to have respect for our earthly Mother and Father and our Spiritual Father and Mother in the God head as persons. Love does not kill anyone. There is only One Power, One Mind and One God. If we know who we are, we do not need anything only God within us.

February 4-This is the Meaning of THE TWINKLE OF AN EYE. We should see the Mind of man changed to the Mind of Christ. The sound of the last trumpet is that we are the Words of God to tell everyone who and what they are. The walls of religious beliefs will fall down at the right sound of awakening from the dream to reality. The dead (all negative thoughts are abolished). No more sin, sickness, death and decay of beliefs from the religious teachings of gloom and doom are resurrected to the body of Light Mortality shall put on immortality. "Death is swallowed up in victory." Hell does not exist only in our own minds. The Soul is awaken see God only. The marriage of the Spirit and Soul takes place.

February 5-YOU HAVE BREAD THAT YOU KNOW NOT OF. The hidden bread that you have is not man made bread. It is spiritual food that is already in you for the taking. This bread of Life is the Christ in you. We need spiritual food each day as well as physical food. This inner Light begins to awaken your inner most Being. The Christ in you is the Bread of Life to feed the hungry.

15

February 6-AVOID CRITICS. It does not matter if everyone loves you. You do not want the chickens and turkeys to peck at you and give you human thoughts. The dead meat that the crows eat will try to feed you dead meat that has no spiritual value. The eagle saints, goes higher in the Spirit where the crows, chickens and turkeys cannot go.

Feb. 7-THE PRESENCE OF GOD IS WITHIN. God dwells in the secret place in our heart. Your body is called the Temple or the Tabernacle of the Presence of the Living God dwells. There are no negative thoughts of ego that Edges God Out. All Life, Unconditional Love, and Peace exist in this Presence. "There is a river of life flowing out from me to cause the blind to see and the lame to walk." I can forget those things which are behind, and reach forth unto those things which are before.

February 8-WHAT IS THE MEANING OF A VEIL? The veil hides the real. A bride wears a veil to show her purity of having no man- made thoughts or man- made rituals. When the veil is removed means the marriage feast of the Lamb and the Bride is ready for the union of oneness. When Jesus was crucified, all human thoughts disappeared and only the Christ appeared. We can go into the very presence of God WITHIN anytime. We have entrance to the Spirit Realm leaving behind the human dimension and going into the very presence of God. We now have the circumcision of the heart (cutting away of the flesh nature).

February 9-TAKE NO THOUGHT. Why do we take thought when the Christ in us is waiting for the request? "Don't be anxious and worried about your life, what you shall eat or what you shall drink, or about your body what you shall put on. The birds they neither sow nor reap nor gather into barns, and your Father keeps feeding them. Are you not worth much more than they? Worry and being anxious cannot add to your growth or the span of your life. Worry is not trusting God. The lilies of the field they neither toil nor spin. If God clothes the grass, will He not much more clothe you? Seek first of all the Kingdom and all these things will be added to you."

February 10-WE ARE THE PIECES OF THE PUZZLE. One piece of the puzzle does not look like anything. The pearl has to have much sand-paper of people that irritates us to make the pearl round and smooth. We are the pearl of GREAT PRICE. The Pearl represents the feminine symbol or the soul realm that is Perfection and Purity. The Christ is that piece of puzzle that is Perfection and Purity. The diamond represents the Spirit part of us as Truth and Innocents and a symbol of our Father God. God is a consuming fire. We are the diamond in the rough when polished is absolutely beautiful. Each one of us has the Christ within us. When we see Christ AS the pieces of the puzzle we know everything is turned into good.

February 11-SHOES ARE OUR WALK WITH GOD. Children put on our shoes thinking they were so big. We hope they will follow our foot steps to BE like God in everything they do and say. Then God says take off our shoes of man-made laws, rituals, beliefs because the ground is Holy Ground." "He who comes after me is mightier than I, Whose sandals I am not worthy or fit to take off. He will baptize you with the Holy Spirit and Fire.

February 12-THE MULBERRY TREE HAS A
SPIRITUAL MEANING. A Mulberry Tree produces a
delicious purple (color of royalty) fruit. God is compared to
the Mulberry Tree that has created us in the image
(reflection in a mirror) and likeness (exact copy) of God.
SILK is made by the silkworm who is a type of butterfly.
The silk worm spins silk and only eats leaves from
the Mulberry Tree. Jesus came to take away sin, sickness
and death and bring us only Life or the Tree of Life
(Mulberry Tree) in the midst of our garden that is within
us. We are becoming a butterfly that only eats the pure
nectar of the Spirit realm to produce the Silk of spotless
and holy life that is God like in everything that is said and
done.

February 13-DELETE WHAT IS NOT POSITIVE. Our
thoughts that are not God like that causes us to have pain
and suffering, we can push the delete button. I can see
through the eyes of Forgiveness. I can see the world
blessed. I can picture in my computer that everyone has
God within them. I AM a unique Masterpiece. Every ego
thoughts that EDGES GOD OUT, that tells you anything
negative about yourself, you can DELETE. A virus of
negative thoughts can cause you to have disease in your
computer. Do you think you can wipe away all thoughts in
your computer that does not bring Love, Life and
Happiness?

February 14-LOVE IS RENEWED IN ME TODAY. This
is a day to renew your Love to each person you meet. "All
things are possible with Christ." We have to overlook
people's faults and see their beauty as Pure Spirit Beings
created in the image (reflection in a mirror) and likeness
(exact COPY) of God. Our most important gifts we can
give a person are to show appreciation, kindness and Love.
Think of every one you meet today as a HOLY
ENCOUNTER.

February 15-DO WE SEE LIKE GOD SEES? God sees everything as a perfect creation in a spiritual world and a spiritual body. We see a physical world of good and evil and a physical body with sin, sickness, pain and death. We are living in a dream world waiting to awaken from illusion to reality. We follow the law of "Love God and Love your neighbor as yourself. God is in us and AS US. It is not "I, but Christ in me."

February 16-WHAT IS A MAGNET? It is certain alloys of iron, natural or manmade, that attracts. The magnet attracts negative or positive things according to its polarization Within us, we should always look for the positive. No more arguments, fear, unloving thoughts towards each other. We attract, Love, Health, Blessings, no more seeing faults, but beauty. We can use the Law of Attraction to bring back to us everything we give out. This Living Magnet attracts only positive thoughts instead of negative words and negative actions.

February 17-LOVE HEALS EVERYTHING THAT IS NEGATIVE. Love heals every imperfection of mind or body. Love overcomes hatred, envy, and criticism. I let Love express in me and through me. Belief must pass through faith, into acceptance and by acknowledgment. "Love God with all your soul and your mind and Love your neighbor as your own self." Matt. 22:37-Your real self is your God Self or the Christ.

February 18-THIS IS THE BOOK OF LIFE. You are written in the "LAMB'S BOOK OF LIFE. "I AM the Lamb of God who takes away the sins of the world without spot or blemish. John 1:29- Sheep (thoughts) always follow their shepherd. "There shall be no longer anything of death, impure, offensive or horrible situations and only the Throne of God and the Lambs (all of us) BOOK OF LIFE shall be in it."

February 19-GOD DID SUBJECT US TO VANITY. In Romans 8:20-"For the creation was made subject to vanity (void of the Truth), not willing, but by the reason of Him (The Creator) who SUBJECTED) the same in HOPE, that nature itself will be set free from its bondage to decay and corruption." Our Soul becomes one with the Spirit by the Marriage of Spirit and Soul." Now God is ALL IN ALL INSTEAD OF ALL IN ONE.

February 20-WHY ARE YOU HERE? You are here to learn how Love Unconditional. We create hate, envy, jealousy, fear, anxiety and the list goes on. Fear causes our cells in our bodies to be out of harmony. If you hate someone they can feel the hatred in their bodies. When you are not at ease, it causes disease that spreads to others as well. We must real-eyes how we are all connected and the ripple effect we have on others. God creates Love!

February 21-WE HAVE A HIGH PRIEST. We can go into the presence of God. Jesus shed his human blood with all the impurities from beliefs, religions, sins and everything human thoughts could conceive and brought them to the cross and crucified them. The Oil (Christ) of the Holy Spirit is rubbed on and smeared on the head (Mind of Christ) to the toes (our walk with God). "Jesus in Heb. 4:15-is our High Priest who understands and sympathize and have a shared feeling with our weakness and infirmities to the assaults of temptation, but ONE WHO HAS BEEN TEMPTED IN EVERY RESPECT AS WE ARE, YET WITHOUT SIN (not missing the mark of Being God like)."

February 22-GOD IS THE LOVE THAT CHANGES ALL THINGS. God is all there is. It is not "I" that does anything. This "I" of me was deleted at the cross when Christ came into our lives. The Christ in me writes the lessons each day. Christ is in our Being and as our Being. Truth is this is a Spiritual Universe and a Spiritual Body without the thought of good and evil. There is One Power and that is God. Look at the flowers, trees and people with the eyes of the Spirit and see how unexplainable that everything is so beautiful. God is UNCONDITIONAL LOVE. We do not have to struggle or try to Love. We are Love.

February 23-RECONCILIATION BRINGS US BACK TO GOD. We have our redemption through His blood (Jesus shed human blood) which means the forgiveness of sins. "NOW HE IS THE EXACT LIKENESS OF THE UNSEEN GOD-THE VISIBLE REPRESENTATION OF THE INVISIBLE. HE IS THE FIRST BORN OF all creation. He is the Head of the Body, the Church and THROUGH HIM, ALL THINGS SHOULD BE COMPLETELY RECONCILED BACK TO HIMSELF. AND ALTHOUGH YOU AT ONE TIME WERE ESTRANGED AND ALIENATED FROM HIM AND OF THE HOSTILE ATTITUDE OF MIND, YOU ARE RECONCILED TO GOD."

February 24- NEW GROWTH IS IN GOD. We grow spiritually each day. One Truth can't be put in cement because the Truth sets you free. The worm consumes all of human thinking and eats every belief of carnal thinking. The cocoon stage sorts out what is spiritual to what was man made. The butterfly only eats the realm of Spirit and never eats the dirt of the lowest of man's teaching. We can eat the Pure Nectar of the Spirit realm and study each day to learn who and what we are. We can never stop growing. Awaken to the fact that God dwells in you and AS YOU. It is not "I", but the Christ as me.

February 25-I OPEN MYSELF UP TO A GREATER
LOVE. I want the Agape Love called the Christ Love.
God is Love, and we are the image (reflection in a mirror
and likeness (exact copy) both male and female. .Love
renews the soul of my mind, my will, my intellect, my
many emotions to God's Mind, Will, Intellect and One
Emotion of Love. Perfect Love cast our fear and flees with
the Truth. "Nothing can separate me from the Love of
God." The power of Life and Death is in the tongue." I AM
Love and so are you. Not "I" but the Christ in me.

February 26-THIS IS THE TEXTURE OF YOUR LIFE.
Texture means look and feel of a fabric. The texture of our
lives is to be joyful, happy, and loving. We are no longer
under the law of sin, sickness and death, just Unconditional
Love. The job of the ego thoughts that edge God out is to
try to destroy your perfect Identity as Spirit Beings. "This
too will pass like a rainy day.". No blockage can cause us
not to get the blessings of God in everything we need.
Remember God is in us and AS us. We are the container
and the vessel that God dwells in us. It is not I, but the
Christ.

February 27-MY WORDS ARE CREATIVE. John 14:12-
"Verily, verily, I say unto you, He that believeth on me, the
works that I do shall he do also; and greater works than
THESE SHALL YOU DO." We are the visible
representation of the invisible God. The Christ in me does
the works. I AM the container of the Christ like a carton of
milk is the container of the milk. "We want to BE
transformed by the Renewing of our mind." "GREATER
IS HE THAT IS IN ME THAN ANY CONDITION AND
IT CAN BE DISSOLVED." We can put anything that is
not God like under our feet and walk away and know that
the feet are our walk with God on HOLY GROUND.

February 28-GOD GOES WITH ME WHEREVER I GO. I can't be disturbed by anything when God rests in me as peace. The storms are calmed in my life by reminding me that "It is not I, but the Christ in me." God is my Source, my Vision and my Light in which I see. I have the Mind of Christ in which I think." "If "I" (little self) make my bed in hell, I will be with you." I let my light shine with understanding to those in darkness in a negative world. We have a spiritual body that is able to bring to you peace, happiness and Joy

MARCH

March 1-I AM THE LIGHT OF THE WORLD. Light is symbol of intelligence, understanding, radiant energy which one sees, brightness. You can divide the Light (Spirit Realm) from the darkness (realm of negative human thinking). In Rev. 21:22-"I saw no temple (we are the temple of the Living God) in the city (city is us), for the Lord God Omnipotent (all powerful) and the Lamb And the city has no need of the sun or of the moon (artificial light) to give light to it for the splendor and radiance glory of God illuminates it, and the Lamb is its lamp. The nations shall walk by its light. Nothing that defiles or unclean or is unwashed shall ever enter it." We get rid of darkness by turning on the light. The darkness only exists in our own minds.

March 2-ENEMIES EXIST IN OUR OWN MINDS. Matt. 10:36-"And a man's foes shall be they of his own household." Our enemies exist in our own individual minds from our own thinking. The EGO are thoughts in our mind that Edges God Out. These thoughts try to destroy our perfect Identity as a Spirit Being having human experiences. The thoughts of God says that God within me is mighty to heal and heals me of my disease and removes all fear (false evidence appearing real) from me, sickness, and pain. I can set healing into motion. I AM free of enemies in my own mind.

March 3-PERFECT LOVE CAST OUT ANY EMOTION THAT IS NOT GOD. Fear tries to destroy your perfect Identity as a Spirit Being. Anger is an emotion that causes our bodies to be out of control. Jealously is an emotion not ever necessary. If God is in you, you have everything and need of nothing. When we think we are not good enough, worthy enough, smart enough, and the emotions go on and on, this is a sign that this is not God. The ego thoughts will wake you up in the middle of the night with this foolishness. Forgiveness is needed in order for us to be forgiven. You are a masterpiece to God. You must let the Christ in you flow through you and Love.

March 4-I AM A SPIRIT BEING. God is Love, Peace, Joy, Happiness and the healer of any problem I may have. Fear (False evidence appearing real) goes away as we turn on the light within us where there is no darkness. We are the VISIBLE MANIFESTATION OF THE INVISIBLE GOD on this earth. Clouds are beautiful when they look like cotton balls in the sky, but dark rain clouds hide my blue sky with trouble, darkness, negative thinking, death and unbelief. The Holy Spirit will clear my mind and thinking to the thinking of God. Not "I" but the Christ in me.

March 5-MY FUNCTION IS TO REMEMBER I AM GODLIKE. My function is to bring the light into a negative dark world of good and evil. I can forgive and erase past hurts. My words help others to understand who and what they are. God is in me in everything I do and say. My function is to let God and let go of my will to the will of God. I AM dying to self and becoming alive to Christ. I can be Godlike in everything I do and say. I came here to awaken the souls that are asleep from the dream world to the real world of reality. I know that this is a spiritual body and a spiritual universe that cannot have pain, suffering and death.

March 6-IN MY AUTHORITY, WE NEED TO CALL "THE THINGS THAT ARE NOT AS THOUGH THEY ARE." Romans 4:17. Confess the things you want in your life and not the things you do not have. Say, I AM Smart, Beautiful, Healthy, Abundance, I AM Healed, Prosperous. I AM God like in everything I say and do. There is the Spirit within us that is greater than we are. We are the container of this Substance and not the Substance. "The Kingdom is within." "ALL Things are Possible with God." Hold on to your dreams and let no man discourage you from your goal in life. "Life and death are in the power of the tongue."

March 7-THE MEANING OF THE OUR FATHER PRAYER. Prayer is contact with God. God is supreme, Omnipotent, Infinite, all present. Thy Kingdom come in the invisible and to the visible within us and thy will be done on earth (this body) as it is in heaven or Spirit. "Man shall not live by bread alone, but by every word impartation of the Spirit." Trespasses not having the Mind of Christ make mistakes not living in the highest Identity of who and what we are. My temptation is to believe in good and evil. If you say you are God than walk through walls, heal the sick, raise the dead. This is a great temptation to say you are God. We are the container or temple of Holy Spirit. It is not I, but the Christ in us.

March 8-LOVE MAKES THE DARK PATH LIGHT. I can remember more than one person who gave me Unconditional Love in the past and changed my life completely. Our Mother God, the Holy Spirit, gives us Unconditional Love with a Love that nothing else can compare to it. "Love is patient and kind, never selfish or rude, always believes the best in people, love never fails, always rejoices when right and truth prevail, does not insist on its own rights, takes no account of evil done to it, Love is eternal and never passes away." All negative thoughts and actions fade away like the darkness goes away when we turn on the light.

March 9-MIND OF CHRIST OR THE HUMAN MIND. The human mind believes the lies of the ego thoughts that Edge God Out. This mind says my will and my mind and emotions are instead of the Mind of Christ. This mind is a fighter, "Eye for an eye and a tooth for a tooth." This mind takes a truth of God and says this is impossible. The Mind of Christ is receiving only God's Truth. The selfish "I" can do nothing of its self, but God does everything. It is peaceful and sees a beautiful world instead of a physical world and a physical body. It never fights or tries to be right

March 10-WE ARE TO FOLLOW THE PATTERN. The word pattern means one worthy of imitation; plan used in making things. 1 Tim. 1:16-"Jesus Christ is a pattern to them that should believe on Him to life everlasting.". A plant that has dead leaves on it has to be pruned in order for the rest of the plant to be healthy. You are that special plant that needs to prune old religious thoughts, human beliefs, carnal rituals, and thoughts that are not God like. The only pattern to follow is the teachings of Jesus the Christ. Jesus is the fore runner or the pattern for us to follow and to learn the Truth of our Being.

March 11-GOD TELLS US WHAT TO DO. God taught me how to take care of our first child. The apple seed is placed in human dirt and human thinking to grow into an apple tree. The animals take care of their young. The birds build a beautiful nest to lay the eggs for the baby birds. At the right time they take away the nest for the baby birds to learn how to fly. The chickens lay eggs for us to eat. The flowers grow and give us the most magnificent beauty of colors. The trees and all the plants and grass are dormant in the winter as if they were dead, and then in spring they have resurrected life.

March 12-I HAVE IMMORTAL CLOTHING. Underneath this physical body is our Spiritual body. "For Adam and his wife God made long coats of skin and clothed them." "For while we are still in this tent or body, we groan under the burden not that we want to put off the body, but rather be further clothed so that what is mortal may be swallowed up by life." The prodigal son left his home or his Spiritual body and came to his senses, and wanted to come home. home. The father put on a Royal robe. This mortal body is changed to Immortal Bodies.

March 13-SPIRITUAL REALIZATION. Jesus the Christ never operated after human thinking and human laws and rules. Jesus had Spiritual Awareness at all times. The Christ saw people as Spirit Beings. We see only appearance instead of seeing our Real Self as the Christ of our Being. God is in each person equally. We are puzzle pieces fitting together to make the complete picture of the finished puzzle.. Your piece of the puzzle is the missing link that makes God complete. We are "Heirs of God and Joint Heirs with Jesus Christ." You have all the qualities of God within you as Christ.

March 14-DON'T GIVE UP YOUR DREAMS
God will always give you the way to fulfill the dream Joseph in the bible had a dream that his Father and Mother and brothers would bow down to him. He made the mistake by telling his brothers the dream that made them jealous of him. His brothers threw him in a pit to die and then sold him to slavery. He was put in jail and saved the baker and many more with his dreams. Finally he became next to pharaoh in rank and gave his brothers and family food in a drought. "His brothers meant it for bad, but God meant it for good."

March 15-WE MUST AWAKEN AND REMEMBER. We went to the process to learn our ABC'S and our multiply tables. Now when we spell a word or multiply, we do not have to go through the whole process from the beginning again. Our Spiritual growth is a daily awakening and remembering who and what we are. The most important dream to remember is that the Christ is in our Being at all times and will not ever leave us or forsake us. We are not the Christ, but the container of the Christ. Jesus did what the Father told him to do and nothing of His own.
  Remember this is a spiritual body motivated by the Spirit.

30

March 16-THE TEMPTATIONS OF JESUS. Jesus was tempted three times by what you call EGO thoughts that edge God out or Devil, Satan or Lucifer within your own mind. Jesus did not sin-archery term meaning missing the mark of being. "Turn these stones to bread." Stones represent pieces of the truth and not the whole truth. Bread speaks of spiritual food that is needed each day. "If you are the son of God then cast down yourself and angels will pick you up." The human "I" thinks it is god and does not need anything of God. God has already given us everything with the Christ of our Being.

March 17-LET US PUT ON THE WHOLE ARMOR OF GOD. Put on the whole armor of God that you may be able to successfully stand up against the lies and deceits of the EGO thoughts that edge God Out. "We are not wrestling with flesh and blood, but against the powers of human thoughts, world rulers in darkness and all the thoughts of good and evil that lies in our own minds." We put on the belt of Truth to conceive the Word of God. The breastplate of Righteousness protects the heart to Love Unconditional every one we meet. Shoes are for our walk with God. The shield of faith believes without seeing. The helmet of salvation means put on the Mind of Christ.

March 18-WE ARE NOT TO LOOK FOR A SIGN. Human thinking needs a sign to believe. We have to take the word by faith which is a substance of things not seen, but things hoped for. This substance is Christ. Anti does not mean opposite, but instead of. The anti-Christ is to have a mark in the forehead meaning controlled our thinking, and the mark in our hands of what we do that is not God like. The anti-Christ is not one person, but all that is the rule of man on the throne instead of Christ on the throne.

March 19-SEAMLESS GARMENT OF CHRIST. We are a Spirit, Soul and Body. Human mind thinks he is god instead of the container of God. God clothed us with skin and man BECAME a Living Soul instead of a Life given Spirit. The soldiers cast lots for his seamless garment because it could not be torn in pieces and divided into parts of a human body. This clothing had no human teaching, beliefs, or rituals. The scripture said, "They parted His garments, but for my clothing they cast lots." In John 13:4-Jesus took off His garment of a Spirit Being for a moment to take on a servant towel and washed their feet. "If "I" could touch the hem of his garment, I will be healed.

March 20-PALM SUNDAY HAS A SPIRITUAL MEANING. Palm Sunday is the celebration of victory to have the Christ as our inner substance. "They took branches of palm trees and laid them at Jesus' feet to make him a King." Holy week is the journey of victory that is the beginning of our realization that it is not "I," but the Christ in us. We go pass the cross to the resurrection. Remember the cross was to take away sin, sickness and death in you and as you. We are not the goat to be slain, but the escape goat.

March 21-JUDAS ISCARIOT DID WHAT WAS IN HIS PLAN. Judas was one of the disciples of Jesus that means man not fully redeemed from carnal thoughts or desires. He gave 30 pieces of silver meaning the high degree of perfection and the beginning of the Christ ministry. The precious oil gives us freedom of law of sin, sickness and death. Judas had a change of heart to give the money back. This change of heart is the beginning of receiving redemption to go back to God. Judas was doing his plan and purpose in his life just like Jesus went to the cross with his plan and purpose.Jesus did not have betrayal thoughts, but saw Judas as a friend to fulfill his plan and purpose "Go do what you must do."

March 22-TWO THIEVES ON THE CROSS.
Luke 23:39 "Christ in the middle and within all of us. On the left side was the thief representing the ego thoughts that EDGE GOD OUT. "If you are the Christ (anointed ones), rescue Yourself and us from death." Is 53-5. "He was despised and rejected and forsaken by men. He has borne our sickness and by His stripes we are healed." 'Heb.4:15- "For we do not have a High Priest Who is unable to UNDERSTAND our emotions, BUT ONE WHO HAS BEEN TEMPTED IN EVERY RESPECT AS WE ARE, YET WITHOUT SIN." The other thief asked for forgiveness. "THIS DAY. YOU SHALL BE WITH ME IN PARADISE.

March 23-EAT MY BODY AND DRINK MY BLOOD.
"The Word became flesh (human beings) and dwelt among us." We eat the WORD or the Spiritual food for our growth. The Christ in us is THE BREAD OF LIFE. We take the bread or spiritual food from each other until the Holy Spirit (Mother God) teaches this Truth within our Being. We are the "Light of the World" to bring understanding to a world in darkness of human thinking. "DO THIS IN REMEMBRANCE OF ME."

March 24-LAST SUPPER BEFORE THE CRUCIFIXION.
This is the last meal Jesus ate with His disciples before his betrayal and arrest. This substance is in each individual. Know that we are not the Christ, but the container of the Christ. Jesus broke his body into each of us by breaking of the bread. "Man shall not live by bread alone, but every word of God." He washed their feet to cleanse all of the human beliefs, doctrines and laws that walked in the dirt of all human thinking. "My soul magnifies the God and the union of marriage of the "

March 25-GOOD FRIDAY REPRESENTS A SPIRITUAL
MEANING. Good Friday commemorates the crucifixion
of Jesus. He took away all the thoughts of sin, sickness and
death and died to human laws and rituals or anything man
could dream up. The cross was the cruelest thing that man
could ever dream of to do to another person. The escape
goat is all of us, but the sacrifice goat was the Christ. We
didn't go through the cross, but nevertheless we are
crucified, death burial and resurrected with Christ. We must
throw the ego thoughts off the throne of our lives and only
listen to the Christ within our Being. He never forgot who
and what He IS.

March 26-THE CHRIST IS KNOWN TO ME TODAY.
Life is the revelation that Christ creates everything to
live. I can delete all thoughts of ignorance, unhappiness, all
negative human thoughts with the knowing that God is real
and God is all there is. Spring is here and time for
resurrection of thoughts and beauty of Life all around us.
Let us take the time to smell the roses today, and to see the
beauty in each other instead of their faults. The Light of
God shall shine all darkness of negative thinking out of our
minds. I can be still and know that the Christ is in me and
as me.

March 27-MEANING OF EASTER. Easter is the time of
resurrection of our negative thoughts to the thoughts of
God only. The "I AM" inside of us or the Christ is our
resurrection. This resurrection starts out with
Unconditional Love. .Even nature celebrates the
resurrection of Life Flowers blooming and leaves coming
back on the trees and everything that was sleeping is now
alive again.

March 28-RESURRECTION OF OUR DEAD
THOUGHTS. Jesus the Christ resurrected from the dead
works of human thinking and human laws and rituals and
all human emotions. "I AM" the Resurrection." The cross
has an upward part towards the Spirit of God and a
horizontal part toward human thinking. "For my
determined purpose is that I MAY KNOW HIM AND THE
POWER OF HIS RESURRECTION and be transformed in
spirit into His likeness. I press on toward the goal to win
the prize to which God is calling me upward."

March 29-THIS IS SPENDING 40 DAYS WITH JESUS
AFTER THE RESURRECTION. Jesus appeared to Mary
Magdalene first after the resurrection. John 20:1. Christ
appeared to two men on the road to Emmaus (place in
consciousness where the healing, restoring Love and Life
of Spirit. Luke 24:13. Christ appeared to apostles by going
through the walls to the upper room in Jerusalem (house of
Peace). Christ appeared to Thomas eight days after
appearing to the other apostles. He put his hand in Jesus'
wounds. Sea of Galilee they were to cast on the other side
meaning the Spirit realm and they caught 153 fish and it
did not break their nets. The Ascension into heaven in a
bodily form Eph. 4:9. He is not dead but alive.

March 30-ASCENSION OF JESUS CHRIST.
Forty days after His resurrection, Jesus ascended to return
to the glory of His Father and sit down at his right hand
 He blessed them and was taken into heaven." "You will
receive power from the Holy Spirit. He was taken up before
their eyes, and a cloud hid Him from their sight." John
14:2-6. "In My Father's house are many mansions. I go
and prepare a place for you." Ps.110:1-2-"Sit at my right
hand until I make your enemies a footstool for your feet."
Christ ascended to prepare a place for those who believe in
Him. Jesus is our forerunner. He gives us eternal life.

March 31-WHAT IS THE PURPOSE OF THE SUN? The sun gives us light, heat, energy, Vitamin D that helps all parts of the body. Jesus did only what the Father told him to do. The woman in revelations was clothed with the Sun. Saul was on the road to Damascus to kill the Christians and saw a bright light as the sun and changed his mind to the Mind of Christ. In Rev. "I saw no temple in the city (all of us) for God Omnipotent Himself and the Lamb (all of us) is its temple. And the city has no need of the sun or of the moon to give light to it, for the splendor and radiance of God illuminated it, and the Lamb is its lamp. There shall be no night there."

April

April 1-GOOD MEDICINE IS LAUGHTER.
"A Merry heart is like a Medicine." Proverbs 17:22. A joyful person has a healing effect on our bodies. Smile at someone and they smile back to you. When Love is present, it can heal in every situation. The Christ in us is Love. I look beyond negative appearances and allow God's healing power to work through me. The mistakes of the past can be erased and canceled. I radiate Joy and Life to all I meet. "If you are happy and you know it, your face will surely show it."

April 2-GOD'S GRACE IS GIVEN TO ME TODAY.
Grace of God is unmerited favor that is not earned, but a gift. Grace is Love, Peace, happiness. God's love is present within each of us in the center of our Being. We must dissolve hidden faults, past regrets and future fears. The gift of God is to real-eyes that we are the children of God. We can ask, believe and receive. After knowing that the Grace of God is always with me then I can count of Faith which is a substance that is not yet manifested, but is still there.

April 3-LIGHT, JOY AND PEACE ABIDE IN ME.
We have "Joy Unspeakable and Full of Glory." I have "Peace within me beyond Understanding." I know that the Christ in me does the work. I want the Light of Understanding to be with me to reveal the Truth of my Being. If you want Light, Joy and Peace, think on these things. I can feel the Presence of God with each thought of peace. This water of Life that I drink, I cannot thirst again. I refuse to drink out of the Poison Well of human thinking and human actions.

37

April 4-THIS IS THE MEANING OF THE TWO TREE. The two trees are two different states of our mind. The tree of good and evil is the tree that is in this world of human thoughts and beliefs. We must put on the Mind of Christ. The cross and the temple were made out an evergreen cedar tree. The cedar tree is a perfect Christmas tree meaning immortality and everlasting life. You and I are the branches connected to the Godhead. We know it is not "i" but the Christ is doing the work.

April 5-TODAY IS VERY SPECIAL. Luke 6:23-"Rejoice you in the day, and leap for joy." People are in our lives for a special reason. This person is going to learn something from me to overcome something in their lives. When life sends us lemons we can make lemon aide. When meanness comes from another person, it is sandpaper making our pearl round and smooth. A diamond needs pressure and heat to form. We are that diamond in the rough and with much pressure and fire, we will grow into the person we were meant to be. EVERYTHING IS GOING TO BE ALRIGHT.

April 6-WHO WALKS INTO YOUR LIFE. God determines who walks into your life. Father, Mother God, bless all my friends and family. Stay away from people that are negative who bring you down with their crying on your shoulder. Tell them that you want to hear them say something positive instead. Love is the solution to all our problems. To know that God loves us all the same is so comforting. I can do all things through the Christ of my Being. It is not i, but the Christ that does the action.

April 7-CHRIST APPEARED TO MANY PEOPLE IN THE PAST. Jacob received the Christ and his name was changed from Jacob liar to ISRAEL PRINCE WITH GOD. The Christ brought Abraham bread of the spiritual food and the wine of the new blood. The Christ appeared to Moses as the burning bush inside of him. The Christ appeared to Mary and her soul magnified God. The Christ is the sons and daughters of the Living God. Saul received the Christ on the Damascus road after Jesus' resurrection.
His name or nature was changed to Paul little one instead of Saul ego driven. He suddenly knew that God was in the midst of him.

April 8-THE UNKNOWN GOD IS REVEALED
Acts 17:23. "I came upon an altar with this inscription, "To the Unknown God." Will the real God stand up in our consciousness? God created all things. God does not dwell in handmade shrines. He gives life and breath and all things to all people. You are the visible representative of the invisible God. The little "I" must die and become alive to our True Identity of Spirit. We do not have to ask for anything because we have everything with no lack. We feel lack when we do not know a Living God that dwells within each of us..

April 9-WORRY IS AN ENEMY. When we worry God takes a rest. God is not on the throne of our lives, when we worry. Take sin, sickness, pain, suffering off the throne of our lives. God can change all situations to the good, if we let go and LET GOD. If you are losing sleep, you are not resting and knowing that EVERYTHING IS GOING TO BE ALRIGHT. There is nothing that can touch us unless we let things control us. We can't take other people burdens.

April 10-GOD IS OUR SHEPHERD. I am comparing God as our Shepherd and we are the lambs. Sheep have no defense system. They rely on the Shepherd to lead them and guide them. "We are like sheep that went astray" believing in the human mind instead of the Mind of Christ. The Shepherd looks after their ears to make sure they hear his Voice only and will not follow another. When the sheep fall down, the Shepherd takes his staff and picks them up. The sheep fear no evil because the Shepherd protects them at all times. He leads the sheep into green pastures of life and spiritual food. The Shepherd restores our soul instead of the lies of the ego thoughts.

April 11-YOU ARE A REFLECTION IN A MIRROR. The word reflection means to express or show; throw back as an image. God said that we are created in the image which means reflection in a mirror and likeness means exact copy both male and female. When you look in a mirror you see a reflection of yourself. You will see the most beautiful person in the world as Spirit, Soul, and Body of a Spiritual person. When you look in the water, you will see yourself and no one else. You are the container of the Christ to reflect to the world that the Christ indwells in each of us. "MIRROR, MIRROR ON THE WALL WHO IS THE FAIREST OF THEM ALL? It is You Snow White.

April 12-THIS IS THE GREAT AWAKENING. Rom. 13:11-"Wake up out of your sleep and rise up to reality." We are awakening from the dreams of human thinking, rituals, laws and beliefs with one thought at a time. I awake to the very Presence of God within me and that God will never leave me or forsake me. I can feel the Presence. I awaken myself to be healed, prosperous, happy, and to be made whole and complete. I partake of the Tree of Life and Life more abundantly. I AM God's treasure in an earthen vessel. I AM Heirs of God and Joint Heirs with Jesus Christ.

April 13- GIVE UP LITTLE THINGS THAT ARE NOT IMPORTANT. "Mary has chosen the good portion (Spirit realm) which shall not be taken away from her." Luke 10:42-I know that we are in the process of BECOMING Pure Gold (Deity) when ugly negative thinking is removed. We are not a piece of black coal, but transformed into Flawless Diamond. Pearls with much sand (human) irritation to become round, perfect and smooth. My past mistakes are erased and forgiven.

April 14-GOD ONLY I SEEK. Love, peace, joy, happiness are God's gifts, and are there with recognition and choosing them. I AM heirs of God and Joint Heirs with Christ. Rom. 8:17. There is an Inner Light in us that cannot be sad, have sickness or disease. I AM within me is a hose (Spirit Being) connected to the water (Spirit-God), and I flow with the RIVER OF LIFE FLOWING OUT FROM ME. Love created me in the image (reflection in a mirror)

41

April 15-GOD SEES OUR HEART AND NOT OUR FAULTS. His apostles were not chosen from outward appearances. Peter cursed, Matthew was noted as tax collector not to be honest, Judas was to betray the Christ. We are on the Potter's Wheel daily to learn how to die to the little i and become alive to I AM or Christ of our Being. A baby falls down is picked up and said "YOU CAN DO IT. We are the Light of the world. The light of the day awakens those that are asleep in the belief of sin, sickness, pain and suffering, and even death.

April 16-WHAT IS IDOLATRY? An idol is anything worshipped and adored that takes the place of or instead of God. An idol is thinking in human thinking and listening to the ego's thoughts that tries to destroy your perfect Identity as a Spirit Being. An idol is lifting up the little "i" of our being instead of I AM or the Christ of our Being. "If "I" be lifted up, "I" will draw all men to ME." When Moses lifted I AM, all were healed of all their sickness and pain. Walls are things that hinder our growth and must fall outward to get rid of them. This world is a spiritual world and we have a spiritual body.

April 17-WHAT IS TRUTH? Truth is either created by God or made by the ego (EDGE GOD OUT THOUGHTS) that tries to destroy your perfect Identity as a Spirit Being. This message is sent to all the butterflies that came out of the cocoon of darkness into the light of the thoughts of God. God does not condemn, judge, punish or reward because God sees us as perfect Beings created in the image (reflection in a mirror) and likeness (exact copy) both male and female. We are transformed by the renewing of our minds to the Mind of Christ and shifting from the illusion of the ego thoughts to the Truth of the Holy Spirit.

April 18-LET US ABIDE IN THE VINE. The vine is another name for the root. The Christ in us is saying that we are the branches of the tree and we are also the sons and daughters of God If a branch of the tree decides not to abide in the Spiritual Realm and wants to think he or she is a physical human being than the branch withers and dies. We have to put on the Mind of Christ in order to live. We have to stop abiding in the Tree of Good and Evil in order to be transformed into the Body of Light. We are learning, "It is the Christ in me and as me and not "i" but the Christ." We are Spiritual Beings and live in a Spiritual Universe.

April 19-EXTRA SENSORY PERCEPTION IS IT SPIRITUAL? No, because it refers to the five senses of the human mind instead of the Mind of Christ. Our physical body gives off waves of energy. When we approach a dog, they immediately feel if we are fearful or confident. This is not supernatural, but is a function of our body and our mind. The Spirit within us is always a Higher Order. Some use this energy to intimate or influence others, but it is always a trick of the mind. ESP is a refinement of the five senses, but it is not Spiritual merely a product of the mortal human mind. The Spirit within always speaks in a "STILL SMALL VOICE."

April 20-MY MIND IS SET ON BEING HEALTHY. Our thoughts control our body; being positive helps in healing. Laughter is a medicine. Our bodies are a Living temple (mind) of the Holy Spirit not made with human hands. I have a seamless garment of pure Light that cannot be extinguished, put out or destroyed. I have a healing balm within me that restores me back to the fact that "I AM as God created me." I let every negative thought be released from my mind and let it go. What is inside of me reaches out and blesses everything it touches and brings life and joy to everyone it meets. I AM Love, joy, gladness, happiness and Joy.

April 21-NEW BEGINNING IS NOW. The winter is past, the rains are over, flowers appear, and the season of singing has come. In the spring, you look up at the bare leaves on the trees and all of a sudden the trees are full of leaves. Death is gone and everything is resurrecting to new life. Let my soul be filled with thy Spirit. Renew my mind with the Mind of Christ to infinite abundance of Love, Peace, Joy and Happiness. Let all burdens fall away and suffering melt away like the old snow man with the presence of the arising sun. I AM a new Creation in Christ today

April 22-WE HAVE A SPIRITUAL BANK ACCOUNT. We have a Bank Account of Life, Happiness, Love, and Peace deposited for any situation that may arise. The biggest deposit we have is God planted deep within our own Bank the Everlasting Life and the Unconditional Love to each individual bank. "And God shall wipe away all tears from their eyes, and there shall be no more death, neither sorrow, nor crying, neither shall there be any more pain." Rev. 21:4.

April 23- GOD IS ALWAYS SPEAKING. In a still small voice the Holy Spirit Mother God speaks in your inward Being. The voice thunders into our Being and lets you know that God only speaks instead of the EGO thoughts that are deceptive. I put on the Mind of Christ like I put on a beautiful outfit. My Real Spirit Self is within and is never tired, sick, troubled, bored, filled with pain. I let go and let the "i" in me disappear as the Christ acts for me. I turn my negative thinking to the Christ. Yesterday's disappointments are deleted and are changed now to positive experiences.

April 24-WAVES ARE COMPARED TO OUR LIVES. The waves of the ocean are part of the ocean, and cannot be separated from the ocean. We are one with the Christ and cannot be separated from the Christ even though we are individual expressions of the Christ. If you try to sail on the ocean of life without the Spirit you will have troubled waters of human thinking and human actions. When Jesus the Christ walked on water, it was a spiritual overcoming not just a demonstration. The waves of the ocean can't say they are the ocean, but can say they are part of the ocean. We can't say we are God. We are the container of God that reveals the invisible God to the visible world.

April 25- CHRIST IS YOUR INNER MOST BEING. Your inner most Being is called "Christ. The Christ is the sons and daughters of God. God created the Real Self by extension of His Spirit. Jesus asked apostles, "Who does man say that I AM?" Peter said "Thou art the Christ the son of the Living God." The Christ is that part of us that is God. Our true nature is Christ. It is the power that works in us.

April 26-THE STORY OF RUTH IS A SPIRITUAL STORY. Ruth was a Moabite-the carnal mind pertains to the soul of man and signifies human love to spiritual Love to be grafted into the vine. Ruth represents the daughters of God. Naomi- means the soul when it has failed to unite with God. Naomi means the Divine Feminine or Mother God searching for Love. They went to Bethlehem-House of Bread to renew of the soul and body to the True Substance or the Christ within. Ruth began to separate the carnal thinking to receive only the Spiritual thinking. She found favor with Boaz-God or the Christ and gleaned only the Spiritual Thoughts. The conception of Boaz and Ruth was the ancestor of the Christ within us. We are all the characters of this story.

April 27-GOD IS THE GOD OF THE IMPOSSIBLE. The carnal human mind says that this is "impossible" is possible with God. In the winter there are no leaves on the trees and no flowers blooming, and everything seems to be asleep. Good and evil is instead of God only. We remember and recognize that the Christ is in us and that it is not "i", but the Christ that does the problem solving. Spring is in the air. We look up at the barren trees with beautiful green leaves. The flowers are starting to bloom with brilliant colors. Life begins to resurrect in us. We go from thinking in the flesh realm to thinking like God thinks.

April 28-EVERYONE I MEET IS A HOLY ENCOUNTER. God is in every person whether they know it or not. The center of my Being is God. My name or nature is I AM whatever I AM. God tabernacles (makes home) within us. This is a Holy Encounter and I AM standing on Holy Ground. I must take off my shoes and every piece of clothing of human thinking and manmade laws and rituals. I AM clothed with Love, Light, Life, Peace, Joy. I AM Godlike in everything I say and do. I AM looking forward to seeing my Holy Encounters that I meet today.

April 29-THE TRUTH WILL SET YOU FREE. John 8:36- "If the Son shall make you free, you shall be free indeed." We are so used to chains of unbelief, that we don't recognize the truth. God within us is our Source of perfect health. God makes something real to your Spirit then it is your truth. The appearance of bondage has no power over me. I can dissolve every appearance of false beliefs; rituals, negative thinking, and all man made laws.

April 30-I CAN REST IN GOD.   Rest means ease; inactivity; peace, become still. Peace is like the sun shining through the clouds on a cloudy day. The peace of seeing the stars that light up the night sky with a burst of light. The peace of God in every situation everything is going to be ALRIGHT. Everything I do and say today will be God like. All fear (false evidence appearing real), doubt is cast aside and I feel the power of I AM within. I AM a piece of puzzle that has a special plan and purpose. I can use a stumbling block to be a stepping stone to a higher dimension.

MAY

May 1-GOD'S PURITY IS FREE OF SIN, SICKNESS AND DEATH. Pure means unmixed; clean; faultless; chase. I can change my thinking ego thoughts into God's thoughts. I fill my cup with all that God is to become whole and complete where there is no lack or limitation, suffering, pain, or death. "I let Go and Let God." The moment I feel negative thoughts, I can put the radiance of light on me. I know that God is within me. I AM a reflection and the manifestation of God on this earth as a child of God created in the image-reflection in a mirror and likeness-exact copy of God both male and female.

May 2-THE SECRET PLACE OF GOD IS WITHIN. The secret place must be guarded to not let any negative thoughts to go within. The eviction notice is issued when anything on the outside of us tries to come into this secret place where God is on the throne. We can't let any of the cares of the world, sickness, pain, suffering get in this place inside of us where God is. The carnal mind is trying to destroy us of our Identity as Spirit Beings and learning that it is not "i" but the Christ within. That which is on the inside of us is eternal.

May 3-LIGHT, JOY AND PEACE ABIDE IN ME. Our thoughts create what we experience If you want Light, Joy and Peace, think on these things. I AM aware that the Christ lives in me and is my Being. I can feel the Presence of God with each thought of peace. I drink from the well of pure Living Water that I will never thirst again. The poison human water thoughts are deleted. Gal. 6:7-"Whatsoever a man sowed, that shall he also reap." In my Garden, I can have Unconditional Love. I AM garden has nutrition foods that help me grow spiritually with no junk foods to be found.

48

May 4-I AM ABIDING IN THE VINE. The vine is the root of any tree. The root is God. The branches are the children of God. A branch disconnected from the tree, it whither and dies. Without the vine of Spirit, we can do nothing. The tree of Life in the midst of us refers to the Christ I AM of our being. The Tree of Good and Evil is thoughts towards human thinking and human laws and rituals. If you eat of this tree, you will die to the Spiritual realm to your selfhood or the serpent. The fruit produced by Abiding in the vine is Love, Peace and Joy, Peace, Patience, Kindness, and Love.

May 5-THIS IS THE STORY OF THE CENTURION SOLDIER. The centurion soldier asked Jesus to heal his servant. He did not ask for healing for himself. We make a stumbling block a stepping stone and not letting the situation get us down to the carnal flesh level. The centurion was a man of authority in the physical human realm. He knew that he could speak the words to his men and they would obey because he had the full power of the Roman Empire. Jesus was so impressed by the faith of this man, He sent the Truth of the word forward causing the centurion servant's body to be whole.

May 6-THIS IS MY SELF PORTRAIT. Look into the mirror and see the beautiful, gorgeous, magnificent person you are. You will see a figure of many colors, very unique shining and glowing like a brilliant light. If you can only see the beauty within yourself, you will begin to Love yourself. All the Love in the world must be real-eyes in you. It is very important to Love yourself. I was one who criticized me until the day that God spoke to my heart and said, "WHY DO YOU CONSTANTLY CRITICIZE MY PERFECT CREATION?" From that moment on, my life changed. I AM SNOW WHITE, THE FAIREST OF THEM ALL.

May 7-HOW DO WE PRAY? Prayer is communion between God and man. God is within us. Prayer is union with the Spirit Realm. "Your Father knows what things you have need of before you ask him." Prayer is potential and not begging. Prayer is bringing the invisible to manifestation. We call things that are not as though they are. Prayer is not seeing appearances, but seeing perfect wholeness as we are created. God can only create spiritually. We have a spiritual body and a spiritual universe and nothing of the physical realm. Jesus the Christ took sin, sickness, pain, suffering and death at the cross in us and as us.

May 8-GOD IS THE ONLY HEALING WILL WITHIN ME. Jeremiah 30:17-"For I will restore health unto thee, and I will heal thee of thy wounds, says the Lord." Whatever you want to happen in this world, you must BECOME IT. If you want healing, you must Become Healing. If you want wealth, you must become wealth. If you want Love to come to you, you must Be Love. "Be transformed by the renewing of your mind." Rom.12-2. As soon as we change our thoughts to thoughts that are creative, the body is then renewed. Fear (false evidence appearing real) has no part of me and the healing power is within me.

May 9-BEYOND THIS WORLD IS A WORLD I WANT. I want to take you on a journey in your mind where there is no sickness, death, suffering, no opposite of reality, no sin (archery term meaning missing the mark of BEING God like). We want to exchange this world of duality, hatred, no love, envy, jealousy, a world of time where everything ends for what is more important, filled with joy, Unconditional Love, Peace and God only. This world is everything instead of God. Eph. 4:32-"Be you transformed by the renewing of your minds and bathing in the Truth that sets us free.

50

May 10-WHAT IS THE MARK OF THE BEAST? The mark of the beast is not a BEING to bow down to, but a way of life. Rev. 13:16-"The beast compels to be marked with an inscription stamped on their right hand and on their forehead.". This means the thinking of man which is death is the mark in forehead or in the mind. In the right hand means the right way of doing things that are God like. The number 666 is the number of MAN spirit, soul and body. The letter of the LAW brings forth death, but the Spirit brings forth life. Paul says "I press toward the MARK to win the prize to which God in Christ Jesus is calling us UPWARD."

May 11-No ONE CAN FAIL WHO SEEKS TO REACH THE TRUTH. Rom. 8:21 "If God is for us, who can be against us?" The indwelling Christ is in charge of our lives and sets us free. It is God's good pleasure to give me the Kingdom. I allow my thoughts to dwell only upon the in dwelling presence of Love, Peace, Happiness and Joy.

May 12-LET US GO ON TO PERFECTION.
Perfection means complete, excellent. Heb. 6:1 "Let us go on and get past the elementary stages in the teachings and doctrine of Christ, advancing steadily toward to the completeness and perfection that belongs to the spiritual maturity. Let us not again be laying the foundation of repentance and abandonment of dead works and of the faith by which you turned to God, with teachings about purifying, and the laying on of hands, the resurrection of the dead (negative thoughts) and eternal judgment and punishment. (God does not punish). If God permits, we will now proceed to advanced teachings." God is not unrighteous to forget or overlook your labor of Love to ministering to the needs of the saints as you do.

51

May 13-WILL NOT VALUE WHAT IS VALUELESS.
Mary and Martha are two aspects of One Mind and two
types of love. One is Unconditional Love and the other is
brotherly love. If you do for me, I will do for you. Martha
ministers to the physical, five senses of the soul realm and
the cares of the world and lets ego thoughts rule her mind.
Mary pours out the precious ointment of oil to anoint His
feet from the lowest human dirt thoughts.
Mary means rebellious outcry, bitterness; nothing of this
world satisfies, attends to the spiritual and chooses the
BEST OF THE SPIRITUAL REALM. Their brother
Lazarus represents resurrection life with the resurrection of
our thoughts to a higher level.

May 14-WE ARE ALWAYS TOO BUSY. Our Real Self
(Spirit Being) is not in a hurry, but always peaceful. We
can't hear the Still Small Voice inside when we are
irritated, angry, constantly busy, thinking of being late and
worrying about things that are going to be alright. The
things we can't change, we still can pray. Communicating
with God gives us Spiritual Food to grow. Instead of the
cares of the world, we need to spend time with practicing
the Presence within. Isaiah 26:3-"Thy will keep him in
perfect peace, whose mind are stayed on God and this will
cause our bodies to be healed."

May 15-WHO ARE YOU AND WHY ARE YOU HERE?
You are a Spirit Being. The revelation of Christ in you and
never will leave you or forsake you. You are the children of
God the Father and God the Mother -Holy Spirit. The
Christ is God's sons and daughters as God created us. The
Christ in me is perfect and is everything I need not "i" but
the Christ in me. The body is an individual expression of
the Living God visible to all those that see only the God in
you and to show us the glorious resurrection. "He that has
seen ME has seen the Father." "The Father and I are one."

May 16-GOD TURNS ALL EVENTS TO GOOD. We thought in the human carnal thinking that Jesus went to the cross was a terrible thing, but the resurrection gave us eternal life, took away sin, sickness and death in us and as us. Judas betrayal gave Jesus the Christ to fulfill his reason to come to us. Joseph was sold by his brothers and he became second to Pharaoh to save his family. People who are mean are used as sandpaper to make our Pearl round and smooth. The diamond in the rough brings us a precious stone. We are on the potter's wheel to change the carnal human thinking to the Spiritual thinking of perfection.

May 17-WHAT IS THE MEANING OF THE ROD? One meaning of the rod is for judgment (turning point). We turn our thinking when we see something in ourselves that has to change and is our turning point. The shepherd used the rod as a means of protection for the sheep. He used the rod to check their ears to see if they could hear well. The rod chased the wolves from the sheep (wolves in sheep clothing words that we think is the truth but is nothing but deception). The kings and queens, prince and princess used the rod to show authority and power. The rod disciplines our lives to hear only the Voice of God and nips the ego thoughts that edge God out.

May 18-WE CANNOT CONTROL GOD. The sun arises and sets, the tides come and go, the stars and moon comes out, a seed planted grows up to be what is planted, all these things are out of our control. When we need prayer for anything, close your eyes and see that it is healed and whole, and be a witness to what God is already doing. It is such a revelation to know that "i" can do nothing of myself. The Christ in us heals the sick, takes away dis-ease, pain, suffering, and even death and shows us that there is none of these things in the Spirit that can come nigh our dwelling.

53

May 19- GOD IS A DAILY PROGRESSION OF
LEARNING. The word God applies to the nature of God.
We begin to see that God is Love, Peace, Joy and
Happiness. There is a greater power that is within us that is
within the world. The metaphysical realm which is higher
than the physical realm is still partaking of good and evil
and making mind over matter all that is good. Moses
discovered the secret I AM of his being is God. He put a
veil over his face and did not let anyone know about it
because of fear and ridicule. It is not "i" but the Christ of
your Real Self.

May 20-PEACE IS WITHIN. Part of the cross is to crucify
all external things from you to the resurrection of the Christ
within you. All the turmoil of the world can be left behind
as you choose peace within. The Christ in you calms all
storms on the outside of you. Healing can only occur within
and not without. The Christ never leaves us or forsakes us.
Stop, when things on the outside upset you, and know that
nothing can come nigh your dwelling. Psalm 91-"There
shall no evil or plague, bad weather, false growths, pain or
suffering or anything on the outside come near you when
you dwell in the Secret Place of the Most High God.."

May 21-WHAT IS THE MEANING OF THE WORD
VEIL? A veil is to hide our Real Self. Moses saw the
burning bush within himself and was revealed that I AM
was within his own being. He came out of the Spirit Realm
to show everyone what was revealed to him and they
laughed at him. The veil to the Holy of Holies was to hide
the presence of God that is within so we would think that
God is on the outside up there somewhere. The veil of the
carnal mind called the ego that Edges God Out is to hide
our Identity of our true being as the Christ. A bride wears a
veil to hide her real self as the Bride of Christ and when the
veil is removed there is Glory.

54

May 22-DO YOU KNOW YOUR PURPOSE IN LIFE?
You are a unique piece of a puzzle that only fits in one place, and if one piece of the puzzle is missing, then the whole picture is not complete. No one can fit in another's person piece of the puzzle. We need each other to teach us until the Christ truth is formed in us and is My Truth. It is not you, but the Christ as you. The ego thoughts that Edge God Out can be put under our feet and walk on them. "We are to see things that are not as though they ARE." We are to let I AM of our being flow through us. You are the visible presence of the invisible God to those who do not know God. The God in you can be seen by others.

May 23-WE HAVE FIVE SENSES. We have five senses in the natural, but the pattern is followed from the Spirit Realm. Four of the senses are connected to the carnal mind. The fifth sense has to do with touch, feeling, emotions, reaching out to others. We must put on the EYES OF GOD to be able to see people as Spirit Beings instead of seeing their faults, but seeing their beauty. Let us hear the Still Small Voice of God within. I AM within is my healer. Let not my Emotions rule me and try to hurt me, but will overcome them by nipping them in the bud in the beginning. Let us go beyond the five senses into the Spirit realm of potential where no sin, sickness, pain dwells

May 24-GREEN IN CHLOROPHYLL GIVES US LIFE.
CHLOROPHYLL which gives plants green color, enables them to convert light into energy. You are the High Priest that connects one dimension to another from artificial light to the light (understanding) of God. Our eyes are created to see colors of the Christ Body (the coat of many colors-all of us. Plants are high in oxygen. Chlorophyll gives us growth in the Spiritual Realm because green is the color of all life. We need chlorophyll to resurrect Life of the Spirit.

May 25-WHAT WE GIVE OUT COMES BACK TO US
Luke 6:38-" When we give, we expect nothing in return
with a pure heart." Outside things do not control us when
we go within. Smile at someone or compliment them, and
their whole world lights up for a moment. "Do unto others
as you would have others do unto you." There is nothing
that happens by accident or by chance. Whoever we meet
is for a lesson for them to learn or a big lesson for us to
learn. We can see everyone we meet as a Holy Encounter.
Be God like in everything you do and say
Expect the best to come to you today.

May 26-I CAN ACCEPT THE GRACE OF GOD. Grace
of God is unmerited favor that is not earned, but a gift.
God's love is present within each of us. The gift of God is
to real-eyes that we are the children of God. We can ask,
believe and receive. After knowing that the Grace of God
is always with me then I can count of Faith which is a
substance that is not yet manifested, but is still there.
1 Thessalonians 2:16- "Now Jesus the Christ has given us
everlasting consolation and good hope through grace,
comfort your hearts, and establish you in every good word
and work."

May 27-I CANNOT BE COMPARED WITH ANOTHER
PERSON. You are a unique piece of the puzzle that no one
else can fit in the plan and purpose. I use to compare
myself with others thinking I was not good enough, smart
enough, pretty enough and all the ego thoughts that try to
EDGE GOD OUT, until God spoke to me in my heart and
said, "Why do you constantly criticize my perfect
creation?" We are the treasures of God in earthen vessels
having different plans and purposes just like the human
body with many functions separate that need each other. I
give light to those who experience darkness (negative
thinking and actions.) "EVERYTHING IS GOING TO BE
ALRIGHT."

May 28-MY HEART AND MY FLESH CRIES OUT FOR THE LIVING GOD. Phil. 3:10-"FOR MY DETERMINED PURPOSE IS THAT I MAY KNOW HIM--THAT I MAY PROGRESSIVELY BECOME MORE DEEPLY AND INTIMATED ACQUAINTED WITH GOD, PERCEIVING AND RECOGNIZING AND UNDERSTANDING THE WONDERS OF THE PERSONS MORE STRONGLY AND MORE CLEARLY. I MAY BE TRANSFORMED INTO THE LIKENESS IN THE HOPE THAT IF POSSIBLE I MAY ATTAIN TO THE SPIRITUAL AND MORAL RESURRECTION FROM AMONG THE DEAD (dead to the little self and alive in Christ) WHILE IN THIS BODY."

May 29-GOD IS DIALING YOUR NUMBER. God is calling you. Is your line too busy with the cares of the world, obeying the carnal mind with nonsense, partaking of the realm of good and evil, and using only the five senses instead of going higher in the Spirit realm? We forget God is always waiting for us to pick up the phone and listen to the still small voice in our ears. The word Emmanuel means God is in us and with us at all times. Jesus the Christ came to reveal to us that we are the Christ of the Living God, also. We think we are physical Beings instead of Spiritual Beings living in a Spiritual Universe. Your Identity is the Christ that will never leave you or forsake you.

May 30-YOU CAN HAVE WHAT IT TAKES. These thoughts are just thoughts that can be dismissed and not acted on. When we choose to act on them, God will guide us and our life will flow with the right people in the right place time Every challenge turns out to be a blessing for our growth and things turn out ALRIGHT. You are the visible manifestation of the invisible God. We are the family of God both sons and daughters. We can call things into existence by believing it can happen. You HAVE WHAT IT TAKES.

May 31-"HE IS MY REFUGE AND MY FORTRESS; MY GOD, IN HIM WILL I TRUST." Ps. 91:2. Refuge means protection from danger. The only place to have protection is the high places in the Spirit realm in our thinking. I can feel the Love of the Holy Presence. The word fortress means fenced place; stronghold. If God is my fortress that means I AM fenced in his Unconditional Love and Protection. In my ego thoughts that EDGE GOD OUT can be fenced OUT from my mind and my thinking. When these ego thoughts of not good enough, smart enough, pretty enough tries to come in my mind,

JUNE

June 1-POWER OF GOD IS THE CHRIST WITHIN.
Matt.28:18-"All power is given unto me in heaven and in
earth." In God's Kingdom, there are no sin, sickness, pain
and suffering. "Greater is He that is in you, than he that is
in the world." The negative thoughts in the carnal mind
can and will be dissolved by the Creative Spirit. "It is not
"i" but the Christ in me." The negative thoughts I can nip
them in the bud. I can give Unconditional Love to be
beauty to every person I meet. God is the power of my Life
today. I AM growing spiritual each day in the image and
likeness of God.

June 2-"IS THERE ANY REASON WHY ME GOD?"
The most asked question is "WHY" when we were pure
Spirit Beings did we all decide and have this thought,
"WHAT IF THERE WAS SOMETHING INSTEAD OF
GOD?" We were lowered into the realm of human mind,
my will, my many emotions and my intellect-thinking like
a human being instead of thinking the Spirit realm of God.
"Man became a living soul instead of a Life Given Spirit."
Gen. 2:7. We partook of good and evilWe create evil with
our thoughts and spoken words. Evil thoughts are called the
ego that EDGES GOD OUT and tries to destroy our perfect
Identity as Spirit Beings.

June 3-TO FIND HAPPINESS IS TO BE HAPPINESS. Your words can bring others happiness or negative doom and gloom? Replace negative thoughts with beautiful thoughts. You are a messenger of Love, Peace, Joy, Happiness. We can share words that God has given us of inspiration to help others know who and what they are, and that the Christ is in their Being. What we give out automatically comes back to us. Laughter and happiness is like a medicine that lifts me into a higher realm of Spirit into another dimension where only Love abides.

June 4-WHO AM I? Gen 1:26- "God said, Let US make mankind (all of us) in our image (reflection in a mirror and likeness an exact copy) and God created man male and female created them." God extended Him-self into all of us from all in one to All in All. "Man became a Living SOUL instead of a Life Given Spirit. "You are the Christ the Son of the Living God." The word Christ means "Anointed Ones." We are the visible manifestation of the invisible God. Our soul is my mind, will and emotions until we see that it is not I, but the Christ in me.

June 5-GOD IS NOT IN THIS WORLD, ONLY THE REAL I OF YOUR BEING. The carnal mind of human thinking is not God's thinking. God is in us. We let God flow through us. The Prodigal son left his Father's Kingdom to ask for a portion of his inheritance. This world is INSTEAD OF GOD. The Prodigal son was in the pig pen of human poison thinking that "i" can do it myself." We are Spirit Beings and the children of God. You cannot cast lots for the seamless garment that Christ in us is. God cannot give you a portion of Himself, but all the Father has is ours. The Father meets us from far off to give us the Robe of Deity, Ring of Love, and Sandals to walk in the Spirit realm.

June 6-WE CAN CHOOSE PEACE INSTEAD OF STRIFE. Strife means a quarrel. I do not choose to be right instead of being happy. Choose not to argue over anything. An argument will not solve a problem it gives the thought of separation from God. It is best to walk away from any conflict to be God like. Don't let the ego thoughts that Edge God out control your life. We can change ourselves to always be at peace. Walk away from someone who presses your buttons. Don't open the door to their abuse.

June 7-WHAT DOES TEMPTATION MEAN
Jesus the Christ was tempted three times by carnal thinking called the ego. He was tempted by changing stones into bread. "Man shall not live off of bread alone, but every Word of God" I AM already in Secret Place of a high pinnacle of God within. I AM already in the Kingdom of God. Whenever someone is mean to us, it is an opportunity to Love. In God there is no pain, sickness or death. GET THEE BEHIND ME EGO THOUGHTS SO I CAN WALK OVER YOU and know that Christ is in control of our lives and never will leave us or forsake us.

June 8-"I" WILL TAKE OUT YOUR STONY HEART."
"The stone that the builders rejected is the head (mind of Ghrist) of the corner and the head of the body. The stony heart is the carnal mind ruling us instead of the Christ of our Being which gives us the heart of Love. I AM the Vine and you are the branches. The branches are the sons and daughter that abides in the root or Christ. Without the vine there are no branches or fruit. Take off your shoes of human thinking and human thoughts because YOU are on Holy Ground. God takes out the stony heart that does not care for anyone and serves itself to the Heart of Love.

61

June 9- WHO IS A STRANGER? One who is not known to you is a stranger. Fear (false evidence appearing real) is a stranger. The EGO thoughts are a stranger that tries to Edge God Out and gives you the message of --You are not Good Enough, Pretty Enough, Smart Enough and on and on. You are Unique Masterpiece of God that can only fit in one place in this giant puzzle. I AM or the Christ of your Being has no doubt, fear or any other strange thoughts and is filled with Love. I AM healed and whole, free of pain and have all the attributes of the Living God.

June 10-WE DO NOT NEED PEOPLE TO APPROVE OF US? I needed approval from other people. I AM finally being weaned off the bottle to not expect anyone to give me compliments. Give all your expectations from people to God, because people will disappoint you. I AM the Masterpiece, created image of God. When people hurt me with their words, I AM learning not to let them take away my Joy, and not to react to their poison tongue. As long as I focus on God, that is all I need.

June 11-WHAT DOES IT MEAN TO BE SINGLE EYED? It means to see God only. Jesus took John (love), Peter (faith of seeing the invisible Christ), and James (crucify flesh to die to self) and took them in the Spirit realm and transfigured before them in his Spirit body BEFORE HE WAS RESURRECTED. They saw Moses and Elijah alive referring to the Spiritual body of resurrecting and transfiguration to the Spirit body that is invisible. I have a Spirit Body and I live in a Spiritual Universe that God created perfect. "Be you transformed to the Mind of Christ".

June 12-I AM GOING TO GIVE YOU A KEY.
Maybe it is a key to a new house, a new car, a new boat, or
maybe the best key to everything. This key is the Truth that
the Christ is in your Being in and as you. Our precious
Jesus the Christ gave us this key to use. We have to open
up the door and let the Christ into our Being. You can only
see the visible representative of the Living Christ in me
because the Christ is invisible. We are crucified with the
Christ, nevertheless we live, not "i" but the Christ in me
and as me." Please open up the door with the key I AM
giving you and go into the world of God or Spirit realm.
You are a Spirit Being.

June 13-I RECOGNIZE MY IDENTITY AS A SPIRIT
BEING. I do not live in a physical world or a physical
body. I AM health instead of sickness, I AM free of pain
and suffering, happiness instead of misery and all the
negative thoughts overcome by Truth. I put on the Mind of
Christ instead of a mind that is duality believing in good
and evil. I put on the eyes of Christ and see a new vision
of Love and Happiness. I do all things through Christ in
me and as me. Be very careful not to use the sacred name
of I AM followed by pain or anything else that is negative
to your health, healing and well Being.

June 14-MY THOUGHTS ARE OF GOD. Your thoughts
of misery, pain, suffering, jealousy and death cloud up the
perfect Love of God. God is the Thought and we are the
Thoughts. We see with the eyes of God and exchange our
blindness with the perfect sight of God and receive our
inheritance to heal others as we are healed. The crow is an
example of human thoughts or the Ego Thoughts that Edge
God Out follows the Eagle until the Eagle goes higher
where human thinking cannot go. We are Eagle Saints that
soars into the Spirit Realm where the flesh or carnal nature
cannot go. We are the sons and daughters of God that
belongs to a many member body.

63

June 15-GOD GIVES US GIFTS. We inherit all that God has. We are like Cinderella, we forgot who and what we are instead of being the cinder maid, we are the Prince and Princess of God. The gifts of God are Unconditional Love, peace, joy, happiness, health and the list goes on. When someone gives you a gift with gold (Deity) wrapping paper and a beautiful bow, are you going to say: "I will put it away for a rainy day? You have all the attributes of God now. Your plan is to learn of the Christ of your Being and share it with others. Rom. 8:17-"Heirs of God and Joint heirs with Jesus Christ."

June 16-THERE IS NO OPPOSITE TO LIFE OR TRUTH. Adam and Eve partook of Good and Evil making God both good and evil. Truth has no opposite. Creation has no opposites. Thoughts of death, suffering, pain have no opposite, so therefore does not exist. What seems to be the opposite of Life is merely sleeping or in a dream state. All thoughts of duality are not the Thoughts of God. Whatever you do in life has a ripple effect on everyone else. We have one problem, and that is the thought of separation from God. Wake up Sleeping Beauty and see your True Self as a Pure Spirit Being, a child of the Living God, created in the image and likeness of God.

June 17-THIS IS THE ABC'S OF BEING SPIRIT. The A is to always remember who and what you are. B Means to BE WHAT YOU ARE CREATED TO BE. C means the Christ of your Being is to be recognized at all time. We need to learn the ABC's of our Spiritual walk The only evil there is to belief in two powers and the belief that we are separated from God. In Psalm 91 says nothing can come neigh our dwelling that is evil. "He who dwells in the secret place of the Most High shall remain stable and fixed under the shadow of the Almighty. God will deliver you from the all evil." There is no chance or accident.

64

June 18-I CAN EXPERIENCE COMPLETE
WHOLENESS. There is a point in your life that we real-
eyes that we are Divine Beings and are tired of the pain and
suffering, the wheel chair and walker and say to yourself, "I
AM WHOLE NO MATTER WHAT THE APPEARANCE
MAY BE." I have a Sound Mind, peace, joy, power that is
sufficient to erase every false experience, make the crooked
thoughts straight. I can erase the unwanted wrinkles. I can
make a rainy day become a refreshing sunshine day and
learning experience in my inner most Being instead of
gloom and doom. I can make lemons into lemonade. I can
have fun instead of sorrow.

June 19-WE NEED TO EXPERIENCE. We shall never
know peace unless we BECOME PEACE and truth until
we become Truth. We will never know God unless we
sense God within our own Being. All the happenings in
our life are chosen to cause us to awaken to what WE
ARE. If we didn't experience evil people, how could we
possible choose not to be like that person's ways and
thoughts? Jesus always knew who and what he was here to
do. Jesus the Christ came to teach us about the Kingdom of
God that is within our own Being. We are a unique
creation that is Like God with our own Individual
Masterpiece and can never be fitted in anyone's part of the
puzzle.

June 20-Wizard of Oz- This story was a dream.
Every person wanted something they already had within
themselves. Dorothy wanted to change her thinking to the
thinking of God. The red shoes had to represent the
Unconditional Love (Mother God). The Straw Man wanted
a brain. The scarecrow scares away the crows or the ego
thoughts that Edge God Out with negative thinking. The
Tin Man wanted a heart. This is the heart of God that beats
to the rhythm of Love. If your beliefs are made of tin, they
cannot change. The Lion wanted courage of fearless and
brave qualities. Lion is the King. The Wizard performs
magic. A little man in his thinking pretending to be
something he wasn't.

June 21-GROWING IS A DAILY PRACTICE.
 Children playing to be grown up put on mother's shoes
and clothes. Before you know it, they have their own
families. What a transition that Mothers and Fathers have
to make when we see our own children being Mothers and
Fathers We sometimes stop growing from one realm of
learning to another and satisfied to eat dead meat day after
day. Then, there is some that has a hunger to learn about
God more and more into eternity never stop knowing who
and what they are. The years flew by and it seems like
yesterday we were just married. Learn something each day
from someone else's experiences or from your own study
time to learn from the Spirit teacher.

June 22-WE NEED TO OBEY WHAT GOD TELLS US TO DO. God told Naaman to wash the leprosy in the Jordan (thoughts of good and evil; death; stinky human thoughts; and everything in this world that is instead of God) The carnal mind that reasons everything and analyzes everything will never believe without seeing. Bathing in the Jordan overcomes death and all of human thinking to cleanse in this inner life stream of the Christ within until the body is wholly purified and completely healed. We must deny the little self in order to be alive to I AM of our Being called the Christ.

June 23-IT IS TIME FOR YOU TO AWAKEN SLEEPING BEAUTY. It is night time and darkness is absent of the light and time for me to go to sleep. No sooner I go to sleep, I start dreaming of sin, sickness, pain, suffering and even death. I AM in terrible pain. How did this happen when I AM the Light of the World? Did I go into a lower dimension and fell asleep to dreaming an illusion instead of the truth? I AM still a Spirit Being created in the image (reflection in a mirror) and likeness (exact copy both male and female) of God. Sleeping Beauty sees the Prince, Jesus who taught me about the Christ of my being.

June 24-THE THOUGHTS OF GOD IS ALL I NEED. Our negative thoughts, keeps us thinking in the carnal mind instead of the Mind of Christ. The Thought of God created you in the image (reflection in a mirror) and likeness (exact copy) of God both male and female. The thought of God has not left your mind, and still abides in you. God is the Thought and we are His thoughts. The secret place of God is within you in darkness and invisible to others in my own soul where my thoughts are high in the realm of Spirit. We learn that it is not "I," but the Christ in us that is the motivation of our bodies. Let not the crow thoughts of human thinking stop me from flying high where the human thinking cannot come. I AM an Eagle Saint, and I fly high above any human thoughts into the Heart of God.

June 25-EXPECT GREAT THINGS FROM GOD. I AM taking steps expectancy and enthusiasm, to achieve a goal. We must be willing to learn and to receive more each day instead of thinking that we know it all. When we are willing to grow, opportunities are waiting for us to succeed. I expect the best in every situation and know that it is God's will in my life to accomplish the highest good for me. I know that everything that I choose with the help of God is in divine order. I must look beyond appearances and know that God will direct me to the ultimate good for me and my family. I open up my heart to receive.

June 26-LIFE SINGS THROUGH ME EVEN THOUGH I
CAN'T CARRY A TUNE. "I sing because I AM Happy."
In the Song of Solomon, there is a Love Song from our
Father to His children telling us how valuable we are to
Him. We are needed by God to set the captives free of all
religious babble or Babylon of human laws and thinking. I
wish to tune our all negative talk, dull ideas of doom and
gloom, end of the world false teachings, doctrines and laws
of humans wanting to control our thoughts. Life sings
through me in a higher tune of Love, Peace, Joy and
Happiness.

June 27-TIME IS VALUABLE AND NOT TO BE
WASTED. My husband likes to be just on time and I like
to be an hour early. One day a lady told me that no matter
where I go, I WILL ALWAYS BE ON "TIME." Time can
never be saved up. The future depends on the time lived
"NOW." Matt. 6:25- "Stop being uneasy, anxious and
worried about your life, what you shall eat or what you
shall drink, and about your body, what you shall put on. Is
not life greater than food, and the body far more excellent
than clothing? The birds neither sow nor reap and your
Heavenly Father keeps feeding them. Are you not worth
more than they? Which of you by worrying and being
anxious can add growth or the length to your life? SEEK
FIRST "THE KINGDOM OF GOD" AND ALL THESE
THINGS WILL BE ADDED TO YOU."

June 28-LOVE IS A HEALING BALM. Balm is a healing ointment or oil. The word anoints means to cause to pour out; smeared; to rub in. Remember Jesus was anointed with the precious oil from the alabaster box. They also anointed His feet to represent His perfect walk with God. Mark 6:13--Anointed oil to all that were sick. Kings and priest were anointed with oil. "THE SPIRIT OF THE LORD IS UPON ME, BECAUSE HE HAS ANOINTED ME TO PREACH THE GOOD NEWS, ANNOUNCE THE RELEASE OF THE CAPTIVES, AND RECOVERY OF SIGHT TO THE BLIND; TO SEND FORTH TO DELIVER THOSE WHO ARE OPPRESSED, BRUISED CRUSHED AND BROKEN DOWN.

June 29-KEYS ARE TO OPEN NEW DIMENSIONS. The word key is to open something that is locked; keys ARE for the computer to write lessons; things that explains as a code; keynote is the lowest music note of a scale. Our brother Jesus who is the King of Kings and the Lord of Lords has the Key to unlock any door and cause us to enter and has the KEYS OF DEATH AND HELL (mental and physical torment.) Jesus destroyed this "man of sin," the carnal mind, the natural man, the ego that edges God out; and the old Adam nature within each of us and sits in the temple of our mind. This temple is not made with human thinking or human hands. He shall put all enemies under feet to walk on, and the last enemy is DEATH.

June 30-I PRESENT MY CASE TO THE HIGHEST COURT. To heal means to repair; cure; mend; to make thoroughly sound and whole.." 2 Kings 20:5:5"I have heard your prayer, I have seen your tears, BEHOLD I WILL HEAL YOU." I COME TO YOU GOD NOT BEGGING OR PLEADING MY CASE, BUT WITH EVIDENCE OF YOUR WORD THAT I MAY BE HEALED. NOW I WAIT FOR THE JURY TO GIVE ME MY VERDICT that my case is dismissed and that I AM HEALED.

JULY

July 1 -HAVE A DAY FILLED WITH THE SUN OF
GOD. The sun never stops shining each day. We need the
sun to see clearly the Kingdom of God coming to the earth.
We have to choose Happiness and Peace if the weather
outside is sunny or not. We must concentrate on the sunny
hours in our lives. Darkness means negative thinking and
actions that are instead of God. Let us turn on the light to
forgive and be free. Darkness is only in our own minds.
When circumstances come that are not wanted, we must
know that nothing happens by accident or by chance, but is
divinely order for us to learn to Love and Forgive.
Now is the only moment we have.

July 2-THE BEE-HAVE YOU EVER THANKED THE
BEES FOR WHAT THEY DO FOR YOU? The bees work
hard to produce honey? Honey is a perfect food along
with Bee Pollen and Royal Jelly, and contains every
vitamin and mineral. Every Bee has a plan and purpose
just like we have and need each other. The Queen mates
once and spends the rest of her life producing eggs
(teaching to be God like in everything we say and so). The
worker bees are all females. Bees feed off of nectar (the
sweet pure Spirit Realm).

July 3-A WORM CHANGED INTO A BUTTERFLY.
The Greek word for butterfly is psyche or soul. Our soul is
our individual Personality of our God Being or Real Self.
The soul when renewed or changed in thinking is the Mind,
Will, Emotions, and Intellect of Christ (anointed ones).
Our worm state or caterpillar eats all day. The cocoon stage
takes only the Truth in these dark moments where no one
sees our growth. This stage is said to be our death of our
human self and the beginning of our resurrection. When
the cocoon is opened into a beautiful butterfly, this is the
marriage feast of the Spirit and Soul. The body is changed
like the resurrected body of Jesus the Christ, and said to be
metamorphosis (change in form).

July 4-I AM GUIDED BY THE WISDOM OF GOD.
Wisdom means understanding, intelligence, skill, and
reason. How the ants know how to build an ant hill; the
bees to make delicious honey? Who taught the animals how
to care for their young? Who taught me how to take care of
my first child when I did not know anything about babies?
I AM guided by the Wisdom of God in everything I do.
The Wisdom that governs the universe knows what to do in
our lives.

July 5-WHAT IS THE MEANING OF THE WORD
LEPROSY? Leprosy is any thoughts of the human mind
that says we have sin, sickness, pain, suffering and death.
God did not create any of these things. We are Spirit
Beings having human experiences. Our minds need to be
uplifted to the Mind of Christ that when redeemed is to
utilize the Pure Life of the spirit. Our thoughts are raised to
the healing power of God. After the Sermon on the Mount,
Jesus the Christ healed a man of leprosy. He did not see
the leprosy. He only saw the perfect creation of God in the
man who thought he had leprosy. Unclean means the dirt
embedded in our thoughts of human thinking, rules, and
beliefs. That is why we have to wash or cleans our thoughts
of all human thinking. I only want the thoughts of God.

July 6-I SHARE THE GIFTS OF GOD. God's gift is
called GRACE which is unmerited favor. It is not earned
but given freely. We are saved (saved from human
thinking to the thinking of God) by Grace. After we accept
the free Gift of God then Faith has to come into play. Faith
is in another dimension. "Faith is the substance of things
hoped for, the evidence of things not seen." Faith means a
belief in the presence of an invisible principle that is not yet
manifested. "I will give unto him that is athirst of the
fountain of the water of life freely." He is Risen (now) in
the Resurrection of your thoughts. Don't put your million
dollar gift away for a rainy day. Use the gift given to you
NOW.

July 7-THE T.V. VERSES THE REAL TRUTH. We get involved with a movie that has actors portraying sickness, pain and suffering and it is so real to us as if the movie was our real life. The actors are not sick, pain and suffering in real life, they are just playing a part. Lazarus has to come forth from the tomb of dreaming to real life of the Living World of God. We must remove the veil of acting and bring it open to the real world of Spirit. We live in the Spirit World of Life and life more abundantly. Dreams sometimes are so real, and then we awaken and find they were not real. We must awaken to this dream state and come alive to our True Self that is in us and as us which is the Christ of our Being.

July 8-THE KING IS LOOKING FOR YOU. God is not looking for you to condemn you, but to restore you back to your true Identity. God sees your disappointments, fears and your tears when you are in the valley state of your physical mind. God is going to lift you up from the pit of the carnal mind to bring you back to the Real World where God is to the Mind of Christ. Just when the caterpillar thinks he or she has no hope (something not seen but still believed) then it turns into a beautiful butterfly forgetting about the cares of the world's problems and only interested in Being God Like. In the cocoon stage you sort out what is God and Spirit and what is man- made and the carnal mind. You are a beautiful butterfly that only is Pure Spirit Being that God Loves.

July 9-TWO THIEVES ON THE CROSS. The two thieves on the cross are: Tree of good and evil or Tree of Life; carnal mind (Judas) and the Mind of Christ; life and death; Old Testament and New Testament; Material realm and Spiritual realm. God of this world and the Christ of our Being; Adam and Christ; Sprit and flesh; human thinking and God thinking; The world instead of God and the Real World; The little I of self or the Real Self; Jealousy and Forgiveness. Hate or Love; Love of God or love of money; Voice of man or the Voice of Holy Spirit.

July 10-COME LET ME HEAL YOU. Only your own thoughts can hurt you, if you let them. There is no power outside of you that can make you ill, sad, weak or have pain. We must lay down our thoughts of pain, judgment and fear and never pick them up again. We can choose instead of pain, joy, our holiness instead of sin, and peace of God instead of conflict and war. We turn on the Light, all darkness disappears. All thoughts of bad news and terrible things in the world, I can say, "What is that to me, Follow the Christ. He heals all my diseases and removes fear from me. The Voice inside of me is saying to me, "ARISE AND WALK" for I AM healed.

July 11-THE BRANCH AND THE VINE ARE UNITED. John 15:4-"As the branch cannot bear fruit of itself, except it abide in the vine; no more can you, except you abide in Me." The Vine is referred to the root of any tree. We partook of the Tree of Good and Evil (realm) making God both good and evil. The branches refer to all of us and Christ being the first branch to produce much fruit and it is referred to an almond branch. The branches have to be pruned of negative thinking and anything that is not created by God or Godly thoughts must be removed.

76

July 12-THE DEATH OF THE FIRST BORN.
The first born is the ego thoughts that edge God out and
tries to be on the throne of your mind instead of the Mind
of Christ. Pharaoh represents the ego of our carnal human
thinking. He did not want to Let My People Go. People are
the ones that acknowledge the Christ of their Being. First
Born child or the ego child that does not exist must die and
only the Christ must BE. We must stop the dripping faucet
of the ego mind that never stops dripping negative thoughts
and actions. Turn off the faucet and fix the leak to Living
Waters.

July 13-STEPS TO FOLLOW INTO THE SPIRIT
REALM. Emmanuel means God in us. Sacrifice your will
to God's will. Receiving the revelation of the Christ is
within. To receive the blood not literal but the Spirit of God
on door post, head or Mind of Christ and on each side of
body to receive the Life of Christ in your whole being. Let
the first born die of the ego thoughts that tries to destroy
you as a Spirit Being. Egypt thoughts of the human mind
cannot enter into the house of God. "You are the temple of
God or one of the mansions that God dwells in." Obey only
the Still Small Voice within and having no human power or
authority to enter. You cannot control the Christ in you, but
to be led by the Christ.

July 14-YOU WANT TO ANCHOR YOUR LIFE IN HOPE. Hope is something you believe in the invisible to know it will come to be visible whether or not it happens right now. We have a God of the impossible. An anchor in a boat is used to keep your boat to rest in a safe place without drifting away to the unknown. We want to anchor in Love, Peace, Happiness and Joy. When we lift up the anchor, we drift into negative thinking, this will never happen. It is not "WHY" this happened, but what AM I going to learn through this situation. We learn that God is with us and never will leave us or forsake us.

July 15-ONLY MY OWN THOUGHTS CAN HURT ME. Attack another is to attack yourself. We go through death and the cross, but the resurrection side of the cross is for now Jesus wrote on the ground when everyone was condemning the woman in adultery. I think He was making a circle and bringing to mind all their sins of missing the mark of Being God like. "The Law of Love God and Love your neighbor as yourself is the Law of Life." The Key to Love is to Love Yourself first so you can Love others. Forgive immediately to set yourself and the other person free. Jesus the Christ was not affected in His thoughts when they called Him names. "Father forgive them, they know not what they do.

July 16-THE PRIEST TRIES TO TRAP JESUS WITH QUESTIONS. When Jesus entered Jerusalem at the time of the Passover, he had much public support. The chief priest, scribes and the elders, fearing the loss of their wealth, power and authority, confronted Him. They ask clever questions hoping to trap Jesus, but when they failed, they were silent. They never thought to ask Jesus how they could be like Him. What can I do to be Christ like in everything I do and say? Teach me how to be like you? I know I have to go higher in the Spirit realm where there is no pain or suffering.

July 17-ONLY MY CONDEMNATION INJURES ME.
Condemn means disapprove of; declare guilty; to doom;
declare unfit. The ego can condemn you with your own
ego thoughts that try to destroy your perfect Identity as a
Spirit Being with your own mind, will, emotions and
intellect. The ego thoughts that edge God out told me that I
was not good enough, smart enough, pretty enough, and the
list went on and on. One day, I heard a Still Small Voice
within me that said, "Why do you constantly criticize my
perfect creation? This voice inside of me changed my life
to be able to speak to anyone without feeling inferior, and
to know that we are all equal as far as value to God. The
inner life shines through my thinking and feeling and I see
beauty instead of faults.

July 18-WHAT IS THE MEANING OF FASTING?
Fasting is not fasting from food. Fasting is to dissolve
bands of heavy burdens. Fast from false concepts of what
we think God is. I AM sick means God is not here. No
sickness in God. Yes, receive the Christ within. We fast
from mortality to resurrection of immortality. I can now
walk in heavenly places. There is only Christ. I fast from
me, my and the little i. It is not the human mind made flesh.
Only the Christ became flesh and dwelled among us.
The Father's will be done on earth as it is in heaven. The
unleavened bread is the Word of God with no human added
to and human beliefs. I AM ready for the resurrection.

July 19-GOD'S PEACE IS THE ONLY PEACE TO RECEIVE. Peace is freedom from war and strife. Peace is not in this world of good and evil. Peace is within me and in you because the Christ is within me and within you. I rest in the security and peace. I can radiate this brilliant light that brightens my path to others for them to understand the Truth of their Being. I can trust in God to know that everything is going to be ALRIGHT. God is in control of every situation in my life. You can choose peace beyond understanding today right where you ARE. Where you walk is Holy Ground.

July 20-I AM SITTING AT THE FEET OF THE MASTER. The story of the manic "They found him clothed, and in his right mind, sitting at the feet of the Master." We are the manic (very insane person, mentally ill with human thoughts of much confusion) when Christ passes by, he finds us in death clothes wrapped in bondage of dead thoughts, fears, and ego thoughts that edge God out. We have dirty rags of personal beliefs that must fall away, and then clothed in the Mind of Christ. The manic thoughts are cast from you and drowned in the Dead Sea that can never be alive again, and you are a new person in Christ.

July 21-WHAT DOES IT MEAN TO SAY HEAVEN AND EARTH WILL PASS AWAY? This does not mean the Real World of God. It means the human thinking, mind, beliefs, rituals, laws and anything of mortality instead of immortality. It is the word of God received within that no one person can take away from us. The Spirit realm was left by Adam and Eve and not God commanding them to leave the Garden of Eden. Anything that God did not create will pass away of any human thoughts and actions. We do not have good and evil. It is only God. I die each day to the little i and become alive to I AM of my Being.

July 22-I WANT THE NATURE OF GOD. The name of Jesus the Christ is the nature of Christ. Unconditional Love is to Love God and your neighbor as your Real Self. We are learning to die to self and with the death and burial to receive the resurrection. God sees us as "His Perfect Creation." To be God like is to have no anger; not to take others beliefs away from them, but give them something greater; be an example to others; do not judge others because you have not walked their walk and know what God is doing in their lives to bring them back to God where they belong.

July 23-MY NEGATIVE THOUGHTS CAN BE DELETED FOREVER. Rom. 12:2-"Be you transformed (changed) by the renewal of your mind." The body is a puppet and is controlled by our thoughts. Anything that follows I AM can be accomplished. This thought can be applied to any negative thoughts that the ego thought system that edges God out, and tries to destroy your perfect Spirit Being." Today is a new beginning, new thoughts and I live this moment with God's presence and only God's thoughts We can cancel or delete any negative thoughts or words that we speak." I Can will accomplish all that there is.

81

July 24-GOD DOES COMMUNICATE TO US IN THIS WORLD. I know God is Omniscient-knowing all, Omnipresent-present everywhere, and Omnipotent-all powerful. Jesus the Christ asked the Father what to do. The still small voice in us is the Holy Spirit-our Mother God tells us there is a better way than this to follow the Christ in us. I know that God is in control of my life. God is teaching me to go higher in the Spirit realm where no sin, sickness, pain and suffering exist. Remember the words Ask, Seek and Knock, and keep on asking and the door will be open for you to go in.

July 25-CIVILIZED TOLERANCE- 1 John 3:2 "Beloved, now we are children of God and it has not appeared as yet what we shall be. We know that, when He appears, we shall be like Him because we shall see Him just as He IS." In our present state, we all see God through a different pair of eyes. How can we trust this mind to see God as He truly is? Isaiah 9:7 "The increase of His government there will be no end." The point is, how we see God through our human eyes is unique to us, and we should be civilized and tolerant enough to accept how others see " When this universe was spoken into existence, is spoken out of existence, we can only dream of what will replace it.

July 26-PEOPLE IN YOUR OWN HOUSEHOLD DO NOT SEE YOUR BEAUTY. In Jesus' own home town, He could not perform miracle because of their unbelief. When you make furniture and things with wood, the value is wonderful. Jesus the Christ went far beyond being a carpenter from Nazareth. He taught us about the Christ of our Being. We can only pray that the members of our own family to be revealed the Christ in them, also. If you want Love, you become Love, Peace, Joy and Happiness. We must real-eyes that our family is so precious to us, but much more precious to God. Without our family members, God cannot be complete because God is in us whether we know it or not.

July 27-I AM A SPIRIT BEING HAVING HUMAN EXPERIENCES. Eph. 4:24--"Put on the new man, which after God is created in righteousness and true holiness." Your Real Self is your Spirit, Soul (God's will, emotion and unconditional love) and a body that is the manifestation of the Invisible God. You are the children of the living Godhead. You are God's Treasure. You are the Pearl of Great Price. You are the Prince and Princess of God. You are the reflection of the Godhead. You are Love Perfected. You are the Tabernacle of God or the dwelling place of God within. You are the diamond in the rough.

83

July 28-WHAT IS THE MEANING OF THE DOVE? The Dove is associated with the feminine aspect of God, Love and Peace. Doves carry messengers from God. The Holy Spirit is the Voice of God. Noah sent a dove out and the dove came back to him and found no place to roost because the waters had only human consciousness and human thinking on the face of the land. Noah sent out the Dove the second time and the dove came back with the olive branch of redemption (Brought back to the Spirit realm), peace and resolution "You are beautiful my Love! You have dove eyes of love and peace." When Christ was baptized the Holy Spirit descended on him in the form of a dove. Doves mate for life meaning the marriage of the Spirit and the Soul.

July 29-WHAT IS THE MEANING OF GETHSEMANE? It means oil press; a press for extracting ointments. Gethsemane is the garden where olive trees are grown. Jacob wrestled with the angel messenger until he learned about the Christ in him and then he walked differently with God. "Surely God must be in this place." When olives are pressed the first oil that comes forth is the most precious. The press is a sign of trials, distress, agony, but the oil that is produced is the Spirit Realm. Extra virgin olive oil has many benefits to our physical body.

July 30- THE GLORY OF GOD IS WITHIN ME. The word glory means, praise, fame, splendor, adornment and beauty. Why do I constantly seek the glory of God within me when God is in me always? The Identity Theft already happened. The lower realm of thinking caused us to listening to lies of doom and gloom of the ego. We take off our shoes of human thinking and human laws. We are the SLEEPING BEAUTY awaiting the kiss from the Prince Jesus.

July 31-WHAT IS THE MEANING OF STONES? Stones are pieces of the Truth. Women were stoned to death when they heard from God and were called witches. Jesus calls us LIVING STONES. "Who has no sin (archery term meaning missing the mark of Being God like) cast the first stone." If you ask for bread (more Spiritual Truth), you will not get a stone. You are Living Stones precious in God's sight built into a spiritual house (God within). You are a Diamond in the rough and the Pearl of great price. "To him that overcomes (not letting anything disturb your peace), I will give to him manna (truths beyond human thinking) and a white stone (purified thoughts of God only) with a new name (nature).

AUGUST

August 1-ALL THINGS HAPPEN FOR A REASON.
There are no accidents or chances in God. God knows
what is best for us. Do not recognize the worst in any
situation. I erase the thoughts that hurt me. Today I want
Miracle thoughts of healing to set me free. I have a perfect
life, by all power, by all guidance, all good and all Love.
We have a God that goes to the impossible. Can you now
feel the Power of your words for healing, or whatever you
need this day?

August 2-YOU ARE A MASTERPIECE TO BEHOLD.
"I have given thee a wise and understanding heart, so that
there was none like YOU before, neither after YOU shall
any arise like unto you." Within you is the Invisible God
with an individual brush stroke on the canvas of Life. The
Holy Spirit goes before me and prepares the way to my
highest good. "We are Sons and Daughter of God, heirs of
God and joint heirs with Christ. You are a Diamond in the
rough that is being polished by much irritation from other
people. . The Potter is sculpturing you into the image and
likeness unto itself both male and female. You are a unique
individual piece of a giant puzzle, and without you the
picture is not complete.

August 3-THERE ARE TWO IN THE FIELD -ONE TAKEN AND ONE LEFT. What does this statement in Matt. 24:40-41 mean? The field is the world. Two men are two different thoughts. One is human thinking with all the beliefs, lies, rituals and everything instead of God. The other man is the real-eyes that the Christ is inside of us and only thinks Spiritual Thoughts with the Mind of Christ. Two women grinding at the mill means the soul-that is the feminine side of us that is the individual expression of God that is controlled by ego thoughts that tries to rule our minds with negative human toil and the cares of the world instead of uniting with Spirit to become one.

August 4-THE DAWN OF THE NEW DAY HAS COME. "Out of Darkness (of negative thinking) of the long night, the Dawn (new day; new thoughts) has come." I will let my light shine and not let my light grow dim with fear (false evidence appearing real). This is a new day with changing thoughts and learning who and what I AM and learning more deeply who God IS to Be like Him because I can see Him as He Is. The Love of God has healed me with Unconditional Love. The past is gone and I face this New Day with a bright shining face. I delete the ego thoughts that EDGE GOD OUT that tries to be the ruler of my mind to the Dawn of the New Day into the Christ of our Being.

August 5-THERE IS AGOD'S POWER AT THE CENTER OF MY BEING. "But seek you first the Kingdom of God, and His righteousness, and all these things shall be added unto you." This Mind within me inspires me and expresses through me. It heals me and causes me to know that I AM a True Spiritual Being that has no sin, sickness or death. My words of negativity must be weeded out of my garden in order to receive only thoughts of God and to let my garden bloom. I have the key to a rich, full, abundant life that opens all doors for me to enter. I need Spiritual Food each day in order for me to grow.

August 6-I AM LIVING IN THE PRESENCE OF GOD.
Do you real-eyes that the Presence of God is within
everyone? Your pain will dissolve because God is in you.
There cannot be anything in your life but Christ (anointed
ones). In your marriage, the Christ in you will say I Love
You instead of arguing. Your job will be wonderful
because you will see God. You will see a person that is
Godlike instead of their faults that irritate you. You will
begin to Love everyone with the Love of God that YOU
ARE. The only problem in your life is the Thought that
you are separated from God. I AM the household of God
and I AM on Holy Ground. I AM in the Secret Place of
God within me.

August 7-LET US GET RID OF NEGATIVE
SITUATIONS IN OUR LIFE. Your life is like a container.
When it is filled with positive thinking and positive actions,
the body is very healthy. What do you do with infection?
You get rid of it. The infection in your life is letting other
people control your emotions. Fear, jealousy, grief, hurt,
envy and the list goes on and on is the poison infection that
grows. Forgiveness is for our benefit to release poison that
makes us upset. When we harbor hatred, the first person
harmed by it is ourselves. The past is gone and cannot be a
part of your NOW. Your body is NOW healthy and
ageless.

August 8-WHICH BRANCH OF WHAT TREE DO YOU BELONG? The branches of the tree are the sons and daughters of God. You must abide in one tree or another in order to produce fruit. One tree produces fruit of Spirit which is Love, Peace, Joy and Happiness. The other tree is the ego thoughts that Edge God Out and produces sin, sickness, pain, suffering and death." This tree of good and evil wants us to believe that we have a human self which can operate and manage by itself. The Tree of Life is the Spirit Realm with God at the center of its being and only lives and is controlled by the Life of God.

August 9-WHAT IS THE REAL MEANING OF HELL? There are many words for hell. Gehenna region of lamentations, place of purifying fires, place of defilement; Hades-not to be looked upon, outer darkness; Sheol-hollow, empty, place of unquenchable consuming human desires. Both heaven and hell are states of our minds from our own thoughts, beliefs, words and acts. It is a place in our human minds that is out of harmony with God. This darkness is the lack of light or understanding of God's word or actions. The fire is to purify us to the point of changing our thoughts of self to the thoughts of God.

August 10-WE HAVE TWO GODS, WHICH DO YOU CHOOSE? There is only One God the creator of all that is in a Spiritual world and a spiritual body. "The god of this world has blinded the minds of the unbeliever that the light of the good news of the glory of Christ within us should not dawn upon them." The word ego means self; conceit; the rational part of the mind that controls actions for only the self. The god of this world does exist in our own minds. God is all there IS. The god of this world brings us sin, guilt, condemnation, pain, suffering and death. God gives us Love, Peace, Understanding and Happiness. We cannot live unless we abide in the vine and letting God be in control of our lives.

August 11-God said, "I WILL NEVER LEAVE YOU OR FORSAKE YOU. Where is God when we are in terrible pain and suffering? I must go within where the Invisible God is. I must go past the crucifixion to the resurrection. "I AM crucified with Christ never the less "i" live, yet not "i" but Christ lives in me." Paul said, "When I would do good, evil is still present in me. "I AM, "Love God and my neighbor as my self-Christ Self." God cannot forsake me or leave me because I know that the human thoughts have been taken over by the Christ of my Being.

August 12-WE ARE NOT ONLY A CONTAINER OF THE CHRIST, BUT MUCH MORE. Moses first learned about the Christ when God appeared to him inside of him as the burning bush, I AM of his being. "Love God and your neighbor as yourself." We now know that the EGO thoughts cannot force us to believe in pain and suffering and eventual death. These things were taking away from us at the cross and gave us eternal life. We see ourselves as a container of the Christ. I real-eyes that the substance in the container and I are ONE. Jesus said, I and my Father are ONE. If you see me, you see the Father. So we are not only the container of the Christ, but the container is Christ AS us.

August 13-HOW DO I GET OUT OF PRISON OF MY OWN THINKING? I have the key to unlock all prison doors by the recognition that sin, sickness, pain and suffering and death was taken away from us at the cross. The only prison we have is in ourselves in thinking, I can do everything apart from God. Christ paid the price to release me and no other thoughts had any claim on me now. The little self is not real, but an illusion. The Spirit of Christ has entered and indwells me and I come forth out of the tomb of death and discard my death burial rags to clothes of blinding light.

August 14-CAN I AWAKEN YOU? I will gently nudge (push gently to get your attention) you with new Truths of Christ in you just a little bit at a time. The Pharaoh is the Edge God out thoughts of your being, "MUST LET MY PEOPLE GO." The Pharaoh hides your Real Self and lies to you that your little self is the ruler. Leave Egypt in the dream of mortality (flesh) to immortality. The Red Sea must be crossed. We then go through the wilderness (a transitory state) through the waters of Jordan (judgment of good and evil into the Life of Living Waters) and plant your feet in Canaan, land of your Inheritance. Christ meets us and dissolves our battles between flesh and Spirit.

August 15-CAN I LOVE MY ENEMIES? It is impossible in your human thoughts to love anyone. Love has to flow through you from the Christ within. The only way you can Love is to Be Love. The Love of God is the only Love. How easy it is to "Let go and Let God. Children want their own way and are very selfish in letting their will instead of God's will be done. God is all there is, and we can let the Christ flow through us like a water hose that has a nozzle to direct the water of Living waters into our very Being. We can love our enemies only if we let the Christ do it as us. Then I and my Father are ONE and not me and God, but only God.

August 16-WOULD YOU BE HEALED OF SIN OR DISEASE? Sin is an archery term meaning missing the mark of Being God like. Sin is missing the mark that Christ lives in you and you are of Royal Family. We are created in the image (reflection in a mirror) and likeness (exact copy) of God both male and female. Our Savior Christ in Love took our place as our last Adam being made of sin resurrected in us and AS us. The law of the Spirit of life in Christ sets me free of the law of sin, sickness, pain, and death. "I have been crucified in Christ, nevertheless I live, but not "i" but the Christ lives in me. We are the children of God that will not lose our Identity.

August 17-SPEAK THINGS IN THE IMPOSSIBLE REALM. Two blind men cried out to Jesus. Jesus knew they were blind in the human realm. He went higher in the Spirit able to heal them. Nothing is healed in the realm of human thinking. Elijah means the spiritual I AM with the denial of sense consciousness to the higher Spirit realm. Give me a double portion of what you have accomplished. Elisha represents the Individual Spiritual I AM. It is the higher consciousness of turning within and acknowledging the Power of God within.

August 18-CHRIST LIVES IN ME. "I will be with you, I will never leave you." I have to turn away from feeling of being lonely, disappointed, hurt, or afraid. All these feeling are impossible when we know Christ is in my being and is ready to direct our lives to all that is good. We keep the communication open between God and me. We are perfect expressions of the Invisible God and we can choose to have Love, Peace, and Joy at all times. I can use divine wisdom in everything I do and say. I can never be separated from God only in my own thinking.

August 19-THIS IS THE STORY OF JOB. God said that Job is a most beautiful person, and there was none like him. The ego thoughts said "If you take your hand off Job, he will curse you. "God gave the ego power to take away all his possessions. Then came his wife (the soul realm not yet united with the Spirit to control our lives) said, "Curse God and die." Job's three friends came and they saw the boils and corruption on his body from head to toe, they began to blame him for sinning or doing something against God. Isn't that the ego's way of trying to tell us it is our fault when things go wrong? Then the Holy Spirit came and comforted him, and he forgave his friends and everything he lost came back to him in double

August 20-CHRIST LIVES IN EACH OF US. I must turn away from feeling lonely, disappointed, hurt, pain, suffering and fear because these feeling are impossible when we know that Christ is in our very Being. The Christ is ready to direct our lives to all that is God. We are the perfect expression of the Invisible God. If we do forget when we are sleeping to gently awaken to the truth that God is all there Is. We can do this by letting the Christ flow through us. Not my will, but God's will be done.

August 21-THE EGO THOUGHTS WANTS TO BE ON THE THRONE. We are not under the law of SIN, SICKNESS AND DEATH. "You are crucified with Christ with death and burial, nevertheless IT IS NOT I BUT CHRIST THAT LIVES IN ME." In order to get to the resurrection, we must die to self. The ego thoughts have a fork tongue. It says, "I can do it by myself." We cannot be duped to believe that something else can control our life "We have a high priest who is able to understand and sympathize and have a shared feeling with our weakness and infirmities and liability to the assaults of temptation, but ONE Who has been tempted in every respect as we are, yet without sin (missing the mark of Being)."

August 22-BE IN MY MIND, MY FATHER, THROUGH THE DAY. When we change our thinking, it changes our life. Let me hear your voice to know what my plans are for this day When I go to sleep at night may all my dreams be wonderful. "All things are possible with God." Phil. 4:7- "Whatever is true, worthy, just, pure, lovely and lovable think on these things," The Mind of Christ does not re-act to people's false accusations. It sees people as sandpaper that is used to perfect us just like the oyster needs sand to make the pearl round and smooth. I can see beauty in people instead of their faults.

August 23-THE MERCY SEAT IS GIVEN TO ME. In Exodus 25:17-speaks of a Mercy Seat above the Ark of the Covenant (very presence of God.) Mercy means kindness; forbearance; power to forgive. Regardless of outer circumstances, we refuse to be discouraged. The Godhead surrounds me and keeps me safe in the Arms of God. If there is something that needs to be given attention, THERE IS THE MERCY SEAT. In the center of me is a Presence that is not disturbed by outer happenings. All things are peaceful, beautiful and good.

August 24-WE NEED TO GO FOR THE GOLD IN GOD. Gold represents royalty. God says we are more precious than gold. One of the gifts given to the Christ child was Gold. This means we are created in the image (reflection in a mirror) and likeness (exact copy of God) both male and female. Yellow is the color of the sons and daughter of God. To refine gold takes extreme heat to take out all the impurities making it valuable and functional. It still retains its color and luster. Gold cannot tarnish or corrode and is a symbol of immortality. Gold symbolizes the soul (individual expression of God) refined to perfection. We are that gold that needs to be refined with much heat and pressure to have the Spirit and soul united in a marriage. The gold rings are eternal love.

August 25-ARISE AND SHINE-Is. 60:1- "Arise from the depression in which circumstances have kept you; rise to a new life! Shine be radiant with the glory of God; for your light is come, and the glory of God is upon you. The Spirit of God is upon you, because God has anointed you to teach the good news. He has sent you to heal the brokenhearted, and proclaim liberty to the physical and spiritual captives, and the opening of the prison and the eyes to those who are bound; praise instead of heavy; beauty instead of ashes; joy for the mourning." "The city had no need of the sun or the moon to give light to it for the splendor and radiance of God illuminates it, and the Lamb is its lamp."

August 26-WE ARE THE CHILDREN OF GOD .We are co-creators with God. I live and move and have my Being in God. Nothing can obstruct or withhold the Love of God within me. It heals everything you touch, brings gladness to everyone you contact. I AM a masterpiece in the potter's hands. I AM the hidden treasure in earthen vessels. "I AM complete and healed and whole." God's dwelling place is within me. We were children of God before we came into human experiences. I have all that God has. "Jesus the Christ thought it not robbery to be equal with God." I AM an heir of God and Joint heirs with Jesus Christ.

August 27-WE HAVE THE MIND OF GOD. God is the Thought and we are the thoughts. Our mind is united to God's Mind as light is united to the sun. Our soul is our individual personality of our Being. We are one with God in thoughts and deeds. We are an individual expression of the Living God. Our minds are united to the Christ Mind like water is united to the waves. We are the body of Christ, and Christ is the head and we are the rest of the body according to our plan and purpose. The human mind cannot accomplish anything. The Mind of Christ must rule our lives. We can do nothing without the Christ in control.

August 28-WE HAVE A SPECIAL PLAN AND
PURPOSE. A Lion is under attack just before she births a
baby lion. The ego thought system does the same thing to
us when we are the weakest and think that we are not going
to accomplish something great. It tries to attach our minds
by saying, "This is not going to happen in your life, you are
not worthy, you can't speak, you can't write a beautiful
article, you are never going to stop the pain. I have a
burning desire in my heart to write, share and teach the
deep things of God. You have a plan and purpose that no
one else can fulfill.

August 29-CHRIST RULES MY MIND. Do you want to
blame someone for your mistakes? It's easy to do, but do
you have anyone to take your responsibilities, but
yourself? We must take responsibility of our own actions
and deeds. You can't say that you made me angry, mad,
jealousy and so forth. We have a choice and no one can
make you do anything "Get thee behind me the ego
thoughts that Edges God Out with its subtle temptations."
"If I make my bed in hell (mental and physical torment),
you are there." "Let this Mind, attitude and purpose be in
you which was in Christ Jesus." I AM transformed by the
renewing of my mind.

August 30-IS GOD LOVE?   Yes, but Love without a name is not personalized. I can't feel love without someone loving me. How can God Love me if God is not a person? Is God energy? Yes, but energy without a name cannot be personalized. Is God Light? Yes, but Light (understanding) without a name (nature) is not personalized. Is God The Word? Yes, God is the Word and we are God's words. God is our Father and Our Mother God is the Holy Spirit. The Holy Spirit gives us Love, comfort is the mediator between God and me, and the still small voice inside of us. Our soul is our individual personality of God within us and AS Us.   We are the Prince and Princess of God. The Father and Mother are called the King and the Queen.

August 31-WHAT IS YOUR INHERITANCE? Your inheritance is your family of God the body of Christ. Father gave the Prodigal Son a signet ring= Father's signature= Power of authority. New Robe=New Spiritual Body. New Sandals =our walk with the new message of peace and resurrected thoughts of God. Rom. 8:22-"We know that the whole creation has been moaning together in the pains of labor. And not only the creation, but we ourselves have groaned inward for the redemption of our bodies from the grave which will reveal our adoption "(Our manifestation as God's sons and daughters)

SEPTEMBER

September 1-WE CAN GIVE ACTS OF KINDNESS. We all love compliments when we do a good joy. Do you know what a smile does to someone? A person in the bank may just have had a mean person to speak to her or him, but a kind remark will change their lives for just a moment. You have beautiful eyes. Don't you want to be Godlike in everything you do and say to another person? You may never real-eyes how you changed a person's life by an act of kindness. Every person I meet is an expression of God.

September 2-I AM GETTING BIGGER IN GOD EACH DAY. Each day I move upward into Spirit consciousness of understanding. I study each day to learn more about God. I let go of EGO thoughts. I AM learning who I AM and why AM I here. I came to reveal our Mother God or Holy Spirit. "Let us make man in our image (reflection in a mirror) and likeness (exact copy)." It is our Father God; our Mother-Holy Spirit, Son-The Christ and daughter- Holy Ghost and Jerusalem from above. There are persons in the God head. We follow the pattern here on earth as in the heavens.

September 3-THIS IS THE BEGINNING OF WISDOM. All conflicts must be settled within. Live out of the center of your Being and are untouched by the laws, thoughts of the world. No labels of the world good or evil. Prayer is communication with God. Go to God as an empty vessel wanting only the Truth to fill your Mind with the Spiritual realm. God's presence is the Peace beyond understanding. No evil can be in God's world. We are not mortal beings, but we are Spiritual Beings and have immortality. Let the little i die and be alive to the Christ of your Being. Love is the most important reality. When we love, we do not see faults or make harsh judgments.

September 4-I INVITE YOU TO THE GREAT FEAST. This is not a feast for physical food or human thinking. This is a feast to taste of the Spiritual realm. There are many excuses not to go to this special feast. I have no time with my busy life. I have a marriage that must come first instead of God within.. I AM involved with all the cares of the world. All this negative activity has me captured with much Love and Compassion. I can sell all of my human experiences to have the Land of Milk and Honey of the heavenly realm. God must be first beyond my job, marriage, and everything in this world that we think has value.

September 5-WE CAN CHANGE OUR THOUGHTS. Prov.23:7-"For as a man thinks in his heart so is he." What we think is also what we create when it is spoken out from the tongue. Thoughts of Love, Peace, Joy will come back to you. We want to reject negative thoughts from the EGO that tries to destroy your perfect Identity as a Spirit Being. Today I change my thoughts to thoughts of only positive and that is the best thoughts for my highest good. When we change our thinking about people and also situations these thoughts changes our lives to Love more than criticism.

100

September 6. GOD HAS US ON A POTTER'S WHEEL.
We are at the beginning a lump of clay (lowest of human
thoughts and actions). I Am put on the potter's wheel. I
feel dizzy with all this spinning. The gray vessel goes into
the fire to get rid of all negative thinking. When we are
taken out of the fire, we must have time to dry. I want my
own will and this paint on me is stopping me. We need the
hot pressure. I looked at myself in the reflection of a
mirror (image) and likeness (exact copy) of my Potter who
created me as a BEAUTIFUL SPIRIT BEING. I AM
absolute gorgeous, pretty, lovely, intelligent and everything
of individual Spirit Being. The Potter shaped me into "A
thing of beauty and a Joy forever."

September 7-WHAT CHURCH DO YOU BELONG TO?
The word church means called out of human thinking to the
thinking of Christ. Jesus told us to build our church on the
rock where nothing can touch us in the human realm like
hurricanes, floods, sickness, pain, and suffering. What is
the rock? It is the Christ consciousness. The first coming
of the Christ was the outer appearance of Christ as Jesus
The second coming of Christ is to remember that the Christ
is in our being invisible. We are an individual expression of
the Living God that people who do not know God can see.
The church of God has no limitations, no man made rules.

September 8-CAN WE STOP TIME FOR A MOMENT?
God is not in time and space. This is an illusion of the
human mind that is Instead of God. When we stop time
for a moment, we remove the illusion, and God is ever
present in a Spiritual awareness. Spirit is not in time. Then
we can heal the sick, open up the eyes of the blind and raise
the dead and change their thoughts. The moment time is
still, we have heaven on earth. Peel off the skin of time and
enter in our Father's house. The skin covering is no longer
the outer covering in our hypnotized mind. Absent from
the body is the Presence of God.

September 9-WE ARE BROKEN PIECES OF THE CLAY
TABLETS. Moses came down from a high Spiritual
experience to find everyone worshiping a Golden Image
Instead of God. New tablets had to be formed to let go of
human thinking to the thinking of God. We are a lump of
clay on the potter's wheel for the Master to shape and form
into the image of God both male and female. Moses placed
the second set of clay tablets in the Ark of the Covenant
along with the carefully picked up broken pieces of the first
tablets. Even the brokenness, God will reshape us to what
we are to be.

September10-THIS IS THE MEANING OF THE BURNING BUSH. Moses began to investigate the deeper Spiritual realm; he began to see a burning bush not on the outside of him, but inside desire to Know God in a deeper way. He took off his shoes of man- made religions; ideas; beliefs, and all material thoughts of human thinking in order to be able to accept Spiritual Truths to his Being. This burning bush inside of us was not consumed, but was purification, cleanses all the dross of carnal human thinking and preserves the Spirit part without destroying our bodies. This Burning Bush of Fire grows into a Lake of Fire where all the dross of human thinking is consumed by our God and only the Created Being exist after the image of the invisible God.

September 11 THERE IS A STORY IN A PICTURE FRAME. Your favorite picture is put in a frame in order to keep it clean. The name (nature) of David is that joy comes from God. David represents a soul after God's heart. Jonah was swallowed up in a whale to calm him down, and then spit him on the shore of protection. Saul was persecuting the Christ. His nature was changed to Paul means restrained; reduced; made small; little or instead of Saul meaning demanding; wanting our own way instead of the will of God. God has a way to put us in a frame of protection even when we want to be rebellious.

September 12-LOOK FOR A REFLECTION OF YOURSELF IN A MIRROR. We see our human self until the veil of the carnal physical self is rent to see yourself as you were created. You were created in the image (reflection in a mirror) and likeness (exact copy) of God. I looked in the mirror a long time ago and was criticizing myself and a voice said (Holy Spirit-Mother God) to me, "Why do you constantly criticize my perfect creation? From that moment on, I saw myself with Magnificent Glory never to be the same again. Wake up Snow White and look in the mirror and see, "THAT YOU ARE THE FAIREST OF THEM ALL."

September 13-ARE YOU ABLE TO FORGIVE THE PAST? We are reborn into the new Life of Spirit. We only live in the Now. The Spirit of Life leads us to fullness of supply, health, and so on. Before you go to bed forgive yourself and ask forgiveness of others that we may have missed the Mark of Being Christ like. We can clear out our thoughts of human thinking. "It is not "I" but the Christ in me." The Word is then made flesh born of a woman. God, Spirit is expressing itself as individual being. There is no laws of matter, disease, no limitation and God is our experience our life eternal. God is present everywhere. The Father, Son-the Christ and Holy Spirit-Mother are one.

September 14-WHAT IS MY PURPOSE? My purpose is to BECOME Godlike in everything I do or say and to re-member that I AM a Spirit Being having human experiences. Forgiveness keeps us from prison and bondage of the poison well of human thinking and human actions. I can turn lemons into lemonade. I recognize life, power, peace joy in everything and everyone. I know that eternal light dispels all darkness of negative thinking and actions, doom and gloom. I can see beauty in people instead of their faults, peace instead of confusion, all sorrow into joy.

September 15-I AM CREATED WITH A DIVINE PLAN. My plan is for me to remember who and what I AM. I go back to God where I came from when I change my thinking. Health, Life, Healing, Abundance is in my plan. I squandered my inheritance to a lower realm of thinking that is INSTEAD OF GOD. "For those whom He foreknew He also destined to be molded into the Image of God. And those He foreordained He also called, and justified, acquitted, putting them into right standing with Him-self, and those whom he justified, he also glorified."

September 16-WHAT IS CONSCIOUSNESS? It is what we are aware of; able to think, awake. Fear is false evidence appearing real is only if we believe in it. Fear puts our human thoughts and energies into a place where it does not deserve. I AM not a victim of the appearances of the world that surround me. God is all in all in me, through me, and as me. and I live in an ocean of Consciousness. Not everyone is on the same level because we all have a different plan and purpose. Our Maker is the supply of Life, Love, Health and Joy.

September 17-YOU HAVE NOT CHOSEN ME. I studied the Bible for about 45 years. I went to a church that taught me how to look up meaning of words, and that I needed tools in order to study the Bible. I began my journey to study the bible day and night trying to learn what God was saying to me. I take a lot of time to prepare my lessons each day. My first scripture God gave me was: John 15:16-"You have not chosen me, but I have chosen you, and ordained you, that you shall go and bring forth fruit, and that your fruit should remain: that whatsoever you shall ask of the Father in my name (nature), he may give it to you." I must reveal my Mother God of the Godhead both male and female. We are children of God both sons and daughters. No child is born without a Father and Mother taken after the pattern in the heavens.

105

September 18-EACH PERSON IS UNIQUE. We are the visible person of the Living God and each of us has a special plan and purpose. We must take all of Christ and not just loaves and fishes, healings and so on, because then we are dividing "My Garments" instead of taking the robe without any seams. "I AM heirs of God and Joint Heirs with Christ." The Spirit is the root that feeds all the branches. David was 13, he knew the Christ was in him to fight Goliath (ego thoughts that Edge God Out. Saul wanted to put on his armor. The five smooth stones were truths that endured much pressure from other human thinking to make them round and smooth that no one can take away from us. In the name of I AM there is power and protection.

September19-THIS IS THE PARABLE OF THE WHEAT AND TARES. The tares are the substitute or instead of the wheat. The tares are the human religious thoughts, the sin, sickness, pain, disease, death thoughts that are not God. The wheat is the thoughts of the Spirit-Christ-God realm within. "A man had a field (our human existence) and he planted the good seed (Christ within us) and the enemy – ego thoughts came along and planted the tares" The tares are gathered up and burned by the consuming fire of God that burns out all the dross (refuge-thoughts =that are not God like), but the wheat will go into the barn meaning the Spiritual realm.

September 20-VERY FEW OF YOUR FRIENDS ARE TREASURES. Proverbs 17:17-"A friend loves at all times." A true friend understands what you are going through at the time without criticism or judgment. Some people when you meet that you know that you are attracted to at once. Most friends have the same interest and are willing to share what they have in common. To have a true friend, we must overlook faults and see only beauty. Be willing to do anything for a friend that can help them. Be the person who greets others with a smile, loving and encouraging, and is always happy and cheerful. I ask God to bless all my friends and family and reveal your deep truths to them.

September 21-WE GROW IN GOD IS A DAY BY DAY PROGRESS. When we grow deeper into the things of God, we have to leave people and fellowship behind in order to grow deeper. Jacob wrestled with a truth that changed his life, and he became Prince with God. Saul saw a great light on the way to kill the Christians. His nature or name was changed from Saul to Paul meaning little instead of Saul filled with ego thoughts. Mary had a change in heart when she was told to conceive the Christ by the Holy Spirit over shadowing her. She then said that her soul magnified the Lord. She knew that Joseph was not the Christ's father. She knew she was a surrogate (One who uses her body to birth a child) to receive the Christ born of a woman.

September 22-DO YOU HAVE A MORTAL BODY OR AN IMMORTAL BODY? I know that this body is immortal underneath the body of flesh. Jesus pointed out to us that the Christ is in the midst of our Being. What happen to the baby's body, teen body, adult body, older body when it grew? It was translated into a new form without dying and burying the body. This is the same process from a worm to a butterfly. Why does this aged body need to be buried instead of transformation into a new form? The physical body is mortal and has to die, but the Spiritual body is immortal and never dies. The same thing with pain, sickness and death must real-eyes that the Christ in us does not have pain and suffering. The Christ in me is perfect without Pharaoh of the five senses that will not let my people go from carnal thinking to the thinking of God.

September 23-KNOWING GOD IS MY ETERNAL GIFT. Jesus Christ came to show us who and what we are. The things he did, we can do. We must go in another realm or dimension to do the miracles that He performed. We are the children of God both male and female. We can be just like Jesus in everything we do and say. We are Love and every action of love reflects to others. I can change negative emotions into Love and Forgiveness. This Love of God inside of me can spread healing and harmony to everyone we touch.

September 24-I WANT THE PEACE OF GOD TO BE
BEATING IN MY HEART. Peace is a state of inner calm
that we choose. Peace is freedom from war, law and order,
calm. Jesus said, "Peace, I leave with you, my peace I give
unto you." The Tin Man in the "Wizard of Oz," he wanted
a heart, forgiveness, free of guilt and pain. He needed
some oil of the Holy Spirit (our Mother God) in order to oil
his joints that were unable to move because a heart of tin.
The tin man yearned to re-member a heart like he had in the
Spirit realm. You are royal blood, Child of God, a hidden
treasure in an earthen vessel of the Living God.

September 25-IN THIS FLESH I WILL SEE GOD.
Job19:26- I often thought what was meant by me seeing
God in this flesh. I now see that this is God appearing as
individual Being and Love appearing at this form.
Everyone we meet is God appearing, as God incarnate,
Love is manifested, and this is healing Christ
Consciousness. The presence of God is the only lawgiver.
God is appearing as regardless of the way I see it. When
you are divinely centered in your God-Being, you are
attentive, ready to respond with Love. We must always
remember our Spiritual Self and release this hidden
splendor through forgiveness, gratitude, bearing witness to
the Truth and practice the Presence within. and let it flow.

September 26-MY EYES CAN SEE. "Blessed are your
eyes, for they see; and your ears, for they hear." We hear
the inner voice of Truth. Is it possible to see into the Spirit
Realm by putting on the eyes of Christ? We can see a
world forgiven. We see a face of true innocence, free of
guilt, sin, sickness, and no death. Our sight is perfect in our
thoughts which darkness disappears. He cured them all. "I
was blind, but now I see." Can you put on the blue eyes of
Jesus in order to see in the Spirit Realm?

September 27-HOPE FIRST AND THEN WE KNOW. Faith is unquenchable belief. Heb. 11:1-"Now Faith is the assurance (the confirmation, the title deed) the essence (substance in concentrated form) of things hoped for, being proof of things we do not see and the conviction of their reality." Faith is calling things that are not as though they are. Hope is trust that what we want will happen. Romans 15:13- "May the God of your hope so fill you with all joy and peace in believing through the experience of your faith that by the power of the Holy Spirit you may abound and be overflowing bubbling over with hope." When God gives us a Truth, no one can take it away from you because you know without a shadow of t we Ask God for the things we a doubt that what is revealed is Truth.

September 28-DID JESUS TAKE AWAY SIN? The word sin is an archery term meaning missing the mark OF BEING CHRIST LIKE. In Is. 53:5- "He was despised and rejected and forsaken by men. He has borne our sickness, weakness and distress and carried our sorrows and pain. He was wounded for our transgressions. He was bruised for our guilt and with His stripes WE ARE HEALED." Heb. 4:15 "For we do not have a High Priest Who is unable to Understand and sympathize and have a fellow feeling with our weaknesses and infirmities and liability to the assaults of temptation, but One who has been tempted in every respect as we Are, YET WITHOUT SIN. He came to save our souls.

September 29-CHANGE OUR ILLUSIONS TO REALITY. Sleeping Beauty is about all of us who are asleep until we are awaken with First Love's Kiss by the Prince. Beauty's name was Aurora which-means the dawn that filled their life with sunshine. The three fairies (tiny imaginary beings in human form) appeared to help her come out of the illusion. Flora gave her the gift of beauty. Fauna gave her the gift of song. The evil Maleficent (the ego thoughts that EDGE GOD OUT) puts a curse of death on Aurora. Merryweather, the third fairy softens the curse from death to sleep. On Aurora's 16th birthday she pricked her finger on the spinning wheel and falls into a deep sleep. Merryweather's gift also included the provision that Aurora's spell will be broken with "Love's First KISS'" "We KNEW HIM ONCE UPON A DREAM."

September 30-I CAN RELEASE TENSION FROM MY MIND AND BODY. Some days seem that nothing goes right. "Let not your heart be troubled." I have Truth that sets me free, harmony and Love. Spirit is my own reality. Every appearance of fear (false evidence appearing real) is a false picture. I AM divinely guided in everything I say and do. I have the Christ vision to see a world that is different from the world I made. I have the Tree of Life in the midst of my garden. I can pluck out the weeds of human ego thoughts.

OCTOBER

October 1-TODAY BELONGS TO LOVE. We are like Hansel and Gretel depending on the bread of small truths to find our way back to Love and our True Home. The crumbs from the Master's Table cannot fill our needs to re-member who and what we are. They saw a ginger bread house in the woods (teaching of human thinking and laws). The Ego Witch owned this house of hatred, jealousy, and negative thinking. The Ego Witch throws a rope around Hansel's neck--the part of the body connected to the brain to interfere with their thinking. She was going to eat or consume Gretel's thinking. The Ego Witch thoughts within us were thrown into the Consuming Fire of God to purge her evil thoughts and deeds.

October 2-GOLD IS DEITY. The Spirit part of YOU is God. We are part of God, but not God. Just like children are a part of the Parents, but not the Parents. The Wise men brought gold to Jesus meaning he and we are royalty. The gift of Gold was to remind Jesus that he was the Christ-The Son of the Living God. Gold is the most precious of the metals. Gold is an excellent conductor of electricity. Gold cannot corrode. Gold can be pounded, twisted, rolled into all different shapes without breaking apart.

October 3-WE ARE THAT INVISIBLE SPIRIT THAT
DWELLS IN US. "You shall walk in the way safely, and
thy foot shall not stumble. I expect something new, bigger
and better to transpire. There is no fear, sickness, pain in
the Kingdom of God. Every disorder in my life dissolves
with the truth of the Christ is within me controlling my life
as I let go and let God. The old Adam cannot be revived or
saved. "Behold I make all things new." The Divine
Presence within me is leading me to peace and freedom.
The decisions I make are not always the best for me. I can
put God in charge. I can know everything is going to be
alright.

October 4-WE HAVE A PRIMARY DOCTOR THAT
GIVES US A REAL PRESCRIPTION FOR LIFE. Our
Primary Doctor (Christ) gave us a prescription that did not
have side effects and said go wash 7 times in the Jordan
River (flowing river if not spiritual can be muddy waters of
thoughts.) Leprosy means a skin disease that has to be
cleansed of human behavior and human laws and thoughts.
This is a simple Prescription. Most human thought would
have resisted this word and said, "No" this does not make
sense to me. Water is physical material cleansing until
water is cleansed by Spirit and becomes "Living Water that
flows from me." "If YOU drink of this water you will
never thirst."

October 5-DO YOU FEEL HOMELESS? A home is where our lives with a family and Unconditional Love with life around it. Do you feel home-sick for our heavenly home? We yearn to go back with no pain, suffering, sin, jealousy, hatred and so on. The ego thoughts are needed to make us perfected. God is within you. You are evolving into unlimited potential. "The dominion of this world has NOW become the possession of our God and His Christ to reign forever."

October 6-THE CHRIST IN US IS GUIDING OUR LIFE. "Psalm 32:8. "I will instruct you and teach you in the way, which you shall go. I will guide you with my eye. We can erase our mistakes and start over and go within to receive infinite intellect, wisdom and intuition. Some fish go upstream to their original birth to lay their eggs. What a remarkable adventure we have to go back to our place in God. We pass over high places (trials), clouds (thoughts that hide the light of God) rain, darkness (no spiritual food) and fog where we can't see the things of God. My inner guide directs me with everything I do and say. I can receive only the best when I hear and listen to that inner voice of guidance.

October 7-I CAN FEEL GOD'S PRESENCE TODAY. God is within me at the center of our being. I know new ideas will come to me because I can have faith in the invisible God. If I make a mistake and get off track, I know that God will put me back on the right path. "I can do all things through God." I AM forever at peace, joy, happiness, love and I real-eyes that God is within me. I know that it is not "I" but the Christ in me that writes these messengers. Be quiet for a moment and feel the Presence of God in your life now? This presence is magnificent beyond anything you have ever experienced.

114

October 8-I SEE GOD ONLY TODAY. I know all things are possible with God. God is in me and one with me. Good is always flowing in me in infinite potential and leads me to possession of everything I need. I know that everything from God can only be good. I can forgive and erase the wrong I think in situations and in people who seemed to be treating me unjustly and rude. The past is gone and what appeared in the past can now be turned into the inner Light of understanding. I now can release myself from any bondage I may have thought was keeping me from choosing peace. I can receive only the best in my life today.

October 9- TRUTH AND ALSO FORGIVENESS SETS ME FREE. Some people have caused you pain and rudeness. I AM free of all negative emotions and actions. I know that forgiveness is a healing to both parties and sets us free from any thoughts that are not God like. I let go of all hurtful thoughts and experiences to be free of the past and live only in the now. I receive a PRESENT with a golden box and a gold bow of royalty to set me free. I can now see how powerful forgiveness is. I forgive myself of all anger thoughts I have against another person. I want to be godlike in everything I do and say.

October 10-I AM CREATED TO BE ONE WITH GOD. God is in me and is my life source. I AM one with God. Just like the human body that has many functions, we each have a special plan and purpose. I AM a unique piece of cloth that makes the whole quilt. A skein of thread has many colors, but has unlimited potential to create something beautiful. I AM the unique piece of puzzle that fits in the whole puzzle that no one else can fit. Every cell in my body is active by the Living God within me. God controls my life and speech and my words that I speak. God is breathing through my every breath.

October 11-WHAT IS A WITCH? A witch is a woman to have evil, supernatural power. In 325 A. D. Constantine said women have no rights, and if they had any inspiration from God, they were considered witches, and were burned at the stake. The evil witch in the story of Snow White gave her a poison apple of thoughts of human negative thinking. "We are the apple of God's eye." The woodsman was to cut out Snow White's heart which is the heart of God within us. Snow White's seven little dwarfs were to give her encouragement and protection to remind her that we are a Spirit Being. Look into the mirror (Perfect reflection of your true self), Snow White and see that YOU are the fairest of them all. The Christ will give you a kiss to cause you to remember who and what you are

October 12-WHAT IS A PIRATE? A pirate robs our ship (our human self with lies. The ship brings us back to God. The ego thoughts always EDGE GOD OUT. The pirate is the little self that thinks it is God. It robs us of our Treasures. "Yo, Ho, Ho, and a bottle of run" is what the Pirate says to your mind. Too much rum makes you drunk to not think clearly. The hole in our being has to be filled with God only. Our soul yearns to be back in the arms of God in our thinking forever. A robber thinks he is deprived of something that you have. You are the treasure of God in an earthen vessel that is more precious than all the gold (Deity) in this world. You are the diamond in the rough that goes through much pressure before you shine with great brilliance.

October 13-WE ARE UNIQUELY CREATED BY GOD. There are no fingerprints and no DNA that are alike. We are uniquely created by God. We are all One with God but have a soul that is separate from anyone else, but united to the Spirit and causes the Marriage Feast of the Lamb. We are created in the image (reflection in a mirror) and likeness (exact copy) of God both male and female The human body is one body with different functions. The Christ lives in each one of us. We are pieces of the giant puzzle that you can only fit in one place.

October 14-ALL YOU THAT ARE HEAVY BURDEN. "Come to me, all you are heavy burden, I will give you rest. I will ease and relieve and refresh your soul. Take my yoke upon you and learn of Me, for I AM gentle and humble in heart, and you will find rest." The Christ in our being and our Higher Self is the Me. The yoke is not for bondage, but to real-eyes the Oneness to each other and the Christ that gives us rest and the Daily Bread of Truth to help us to Love and to grow spiritually. The Mind of Christ can lift the shackles from around our bodies where everything is heavy and hard to do with pain, sickness and death.

October 15-WE HAVE A MISSING INGREDIENT WITHOUT GOD IN OUR LIVES. When you are baking anything, if you leave out one ingredient, the dish does not come out right. Sometimes we have pain, suffering, divorce, troubled waters, and finances; and so on causes us to be bitter towards life from beautiful to ugly. We can change our bitter waters of human thinking and human beliefs. We need the yeast of God to help us rise to new heights. These bad experiences make us to have the right ingredients to grow. God is the governor of our lives and circumstances do not control us unless we let them. "Pick up your Bed and Follow God and walk with the King and Queen, and know that "I AM the Lord Thy God that heals thee."

October16-ALIENS-An alien is a person that is foreign to this earth and the earth customs, rules and laws. That must be us. We are Spirit Beings from another dimension that landed on this earth because our thinking had to be changed from believing in a world of good and evil INSTEAD OF GOD. The god-carnal mind of this world has tried to blind the unbeliever's minds that they should not discern the TRUTH. "For a while we are still in this tent, body, we groan under the burden and sigh deeply-weighed down, depressed; not that we want to put off the body, but rather that we would be further clothed, so that what is mortal, our dying body, may be swallowed up by life with the resurrection." "Do not be conformed to this world, but be TRANSFORMED by the RENEWAL OF YOUR MIND."

October 17-WHO CAN SEPARATE US FROM THE LOVE OF GOD? Rom. 8:33-"Who shall bring any charge against God's elect? Will Jesus, who was raised from the dead, who is at the right hand of God pleading as He intercedes for us? Shall suffering, affliction, tribulations, calamity, destitution, peril sword? For I AM persuaded beyond a doubt that neither death, life, angels, principalities, things to come, powers, height, nor depth, nor will anything else in all creation be able to separate us from the LOVE OF GOD WHICH IS IN CHRIST We have a Divine imprint within us. We have Royal Blood, and we are God's children whether or not we real-eyes this fact or not

October 18-DO YOU HAVE A HAUNTED HOUSE? The word house means a place to live; cover; shelter, the body. "We are the temple of the Living God.". Do you constantly re-member all the past mistakes and hurts that people have done to you that you perceive the past a certain way? We can re-member only the beautiful, lovely times of the past. Don't let your house be built on sand of human thoughts instead of precious memories of a house not made with human hands. "In my Father's house are many mansion or dwelling places. I go and prepare a place (realm) for you, and where I AM within you may be also."

October 19-THE SCARECROW HAS A SPIRITUAL MEANING. In the "Wizard of Oz", the Scarecrow or Straw Man wanted a brain. The Scarecrow scares away the crows or the ego thoughts that Edge God Out. The Scarecrow represents the negative thoughts that disappear with the thoughts of peace. The Straw man already had the Mind of God within him, but forgot Who and What he IS. Don't you want to re-member that YOU ALREADY HAVE THE MIND OF GOD.? All of us go down different paths to find the yellow brick road that causes us to think differently about people and situations. We must find the path that brings us back to thinking like Spirit Beings instead of thinking like human being in the realm of soul instead of Spirit.

October 20-ARE YOU GETTING YOUR DAILY BREAD? We have to go to God each day before we do anything to find out what the Daily Bread is for that day. Manna was given each day and the word Manna is "What is it?" What is it that you want us to do in every situation this day? Moses when he needed water he was to strike the rock once and water flowed out the rock from Living Water. The next time he needed water God said speak to the rock. Moses did not get his daily bread and he struck the rock twice without getting any water. First thing in the morning, we must hear from God what to do. Why do we constantly think we can do things our way instead of God's way?

October 21-I WANT THE VISION SEEN BY GOD. Vision is the power of seeing; something seen in a dream; mental image; foresight. Can you believe that God gave the inspiration to us to form a piece of glass (glasses) for us to be able to see? The cataract of human thinking and human seeing has negative actions that cause us not to see clearly because of the opaque film over our sight. I will counsel you with MY EYE UPON YOU. "Blessed are your eyes, because they do see, and your ears they do hear the spiritual sight of God.

October 22-JOY IS NOT EARNED BUT IS WITHIN YOU. John 15:11-"These things I have spoken to you, that my joy might remain, and that your joy may be full." Did you know that Joy is within you? "The Joy of the Lord is your strength." Stop looking on the outside of us and know that Joy is already here within. "A thing of beauty is Joy forever." Joy is achieved by becoming Joy. You have Joy in everything you do and say. A smile brings happiness to another person. A word of appreciation gives people Joy. Happy memories bring us joy.

October 23-THE HUMAN MIND VERSES THE MIND OF CHRIST. The human mind is very powerful. It can hypnotize others, bend spoons, cause fear, bring up the past and make you have depression, feeling of "I can't do anything." If someone says you have a sickness, the human mind reacts on negative suggestions and makes you believe the false illusion. We must put on the Mind of Christ. There is no form of sickness, pain, suffering in this realm of Spirit because there is only One Power of God. It is not the little "i" in the spiritual realm of thinking. The real I AM is within you, and you can't do anything of your own.

October 24-DO YOU HAVE A LOT OF FRIENDS? A
true friend is a beautiful blessing that is with you through
thick and thin. A real friend sees your beauty instead of
your faults. A great friend is not rude or criticizes you, but
says words to make you feel good about yourself. "I have
called you my friends because I have made know to you
everything that I have heard from My Father." Our true
friend is the Christ within us that will never leave us or
forsake us. When someone rejects us or rejects our
teachings, they are rejecting God within you.

October 25-WE ARE EAGLE SAINTS. "They that wait
upon the Lord shall renew their strength, they shall mount
up with wings as eagles; they shall run, and not be weary;
and they shall walk, and not faint." Is. 40:31 God
compares us to eagles and calls us EAGLE SAINTS."
Eagles have perfect eye sight have the vision of Christ.
They eat only live food meaning no dead beliefs of human
thinking that causes death to Spiritual Truths. The eagle
makes their nest in high places (spiritual realm of
thinking). The hawks try to follow the eagle, and that is
compared to the ego thoughts that try to destroy our perfect
Identity as Spirit Beings. The eagle saints have an inner
yearning to return to Christ. Their wings soar with very
little effort." They know it is not trying, but Being.

October 26-ARE YOU BEING TRANSFORMED DAILY? Ecclesiastes 3:1-"To everything there is a season, and a time and purpose under the heaven." We change in our lives from babies, to toddlers, young girls and boys to men and women. What happened to the bodies of each change? They just went into another stage of development without death. Jesus was transfigured before his apostles to show them he could go through walls and with a thought to be anywhere, and to teach them about the Christ in their Being. The Christ showed us that our bodies will be changed into a glorious body without pain, suffering and even death. This death is dying to the little self and coming alive to the Real Self. The ones ahead are in the cloud of witnesses and "They without us cannot be perfected." This is a process day by day change until we are butterflies only eating the nectar of the spirit realm.

October 27-DID YOU KNOW THAT WE ARE HOLY NOW? Holiness means devoted to God; sinless; sacred. Holiness is a nature of God. My negative thoughts can't destroy my knowing that I AM holy because the Living Christ is in me. Take off any manmade shoes of laws and rules because you are on Holy Ground. The Living God dwells within you. Thessalonians 3:13-"He may strengthen and confirm your hearts pure in holiness." I can feel the Presence and warmth of God within me.

October 28-WE ONLY LIVE IN THE NOW. Matt. 6:34-
"I tell you, stop being uneasy about your life, what you
shall eat or what you shall drink, and about your body, (or
your weight), what you shall put on. Is not life greater than
food and the body (showing the invisible God to those that
do not know God) more excellent than clothing? The birds,
they do not sow or reap, yet your Father feeds them. Are
you not worthy more than they? But seek first the
Kingdom (of God and ITS righteousness than all these
things will be added to you." I can delete the past, and turn
to accept my life as God's life in ME now. I must stop
taking other people's burdens which I cannot carry.

October 29-I DELETE MY THINKING TO GOD'S WAY
OF THINKING. Proverbs 23:7-"As a man thinks in his
heart, so is he. "I AM created in the image (reflection in a
mirror) and likeness (exact copy) of God both male and
female." Gen. 1:27- "Love God and love my neighbor as
myself." Sometimes my life is confused and mixed up, but
I look at "ALL THINGS ARE GOING TO BE OK. I know
God is in control of my Life. I have perfect health,
happiness, peace, no more pain and suffering. There is only
ONE Power, and that is God. I believe in the power of my
own words because I understand that it is not i but "Christ
that dwells in me"

October 30-I AM AWARE THAT THE KINGDOM OF GOD IS WITHIN. This awareness within me is a knowing that no person can take from me. This daily manna (what is it) is daily bread and my strong meat has to be chewed over and over again. "Who do you want me to speak to or share with someone this day? I give up all fear (false evidence appearing real) and unbelief. My birth right is I AM a child of God. I can feel God's Presence within me as soon as I quiet my mind to receive. I have Unconditional Love, Peace, Harmony, Joy and freedom.

October 31-DO YOU WANT THE TRICK OR THE TREAT? The trick is the carnal human mind tries to hypnotizes and mesmerize your thoughts to believe a lie that is not created by God. This ego means thoughts that Edges God Out are trying to destroy our thinking with beliefs and rituals of the past. These thoughts are called wolves in sheep clothing that is so subtle that we think it is the Truth of who and what we are. We are God's children with all the attributes of our God. The Christ heals the sick, gives sight to the blind and causes the lame to walk. It is in control of your life, if we let it. The Mind of Christ is our Treat to eternity.

NOVEMBER

November 1-GO OUTSIDE THE BOX. The box is the ego thoughts that EDGE GOD OUT and does not want you to know who and why you are here. These ego thoughts are constantly waking you up at night and given you fear (false evidence appearing real),and guilt. It tries to make you see a God of punishment, jealousy and a god of duality believing in two powers of good and evil. You begin to have inspiration from the Holy Spirit. The box opens us to another dimension of thoughts only of the things of God.

November 2-MEANING OF WHERE SEEDS WERE PLANTED. Soil means the lowest of human consciousness. The seed must die to self and shed its outer covering. God sows the Word which is the Christ within us. The seed that falls on the road are those who hear the Word but dismiss it, and removes it immediately. The seed on stony ground has no root and not enough dirt, and has no protection from times of trouble. The seed that falls amongst thorns is choked by the cares of the world. The Word of God that falls on Good Ground represents those who hear the Word, and truly take it to heart causing it to bear fruit. The fruit trees yielding fruit after his kind, whose seed is in itself reveals the

November 3-HAVE YOU LOST YOUR WAY? In the story of Hansel and Gretel is they are Spirit Beings. Hansel made brooms. A broom is to sweep our negative thoughts clean. Gretel did all the knitting-putting Spiritual Truths together to follow a pattern. The stepmother came into the house and was disappointed with the work the children did. She sent them into the woods in the world of the carnal mind The children lost their way and dropped bread crumbs along the way that the birds of the air ate the crumbs

November 4-JESUS CHRIST ONLY DID WHAT THE WILL OF THE FATHER TOLD HIM TO DO. Jesus Christ walked on water, stopped storms, healed the sick, causes the lame to walk, the blind to see, raised the dead and many more things He did. If God created these things, Christ would not have changed the situation because He only did the will of the Father. We can do the same things if we let God do it and not the little "i" of our being to rule our lives. In every situation we are to ask our Father "What is it you want me to do today?" "Who do you want the Christ to speak to or to raise their level of human thinking to the realm of Spirit?" I AM of my being can only do what I AM told to do each day. I must let go and let the Christ in me rule my life.

November 5-WHO TOLD YOU THAT YOU WERE NAKED? Adam and Eve were told never to partake of good and evil that God did not create. Being naked is losing your Spirit Body. When Adam and Eve listened to the voice inside of them called the ego, they became a Living Soul instead of a Life Given Spirit. The ego had to blame someone else for its own decisions. "It was the woman you gave to me." Then the woman began to blame the serpent, devil, deceiver of the carnal flesh mind that gives in to the pleasures of self. This was the birth of the little self being god, driving us with fear instead of the Real God leading us on the path of righteousness.

November 6-IT IS TIME FOR A CHANGE. At a certain time of the year, we change our clocks either forward or backward. In God, there is no time except NOW. The whole reason to change our clocks is to save Daylight instead of receiving negative thoughts of darkness with the absent of Light which is God. It is time for a change in our thinking now to the thoughts of God only. Time cannot move forward or backward if the only time is now both past and present. We live in the past with negative thoughts that have to be healed in order for these thoughts not to be in our present.

November 7-DID CAIN KILL ABEL? Cain had ego thoughts that Edge God Out. "Whatever you do to the least of your brother, you do unto Me-Christ." Cain wanted to kill the Christ in Abel because the human mind took control of his life. Seth replaced Abel which was the Christ child within. We are not responsible for our brother's decisions. God has to rule our lives with the thought of what YOU want me to do today to speak or share with someone about the Christ the Sons and Daughter of the Living God to others who do not know who and what they are.

November 8-WHO DO WE VOTE FOR? In any election year, we should go to God and ask, "Who do you want me to vote for that will bring the Kingdom of God to this earth realm?" This year the election is on the 8th and eight means new beginning. Could this year be the year of beginning with all people turning to God for their Daily Bread of the Spirit realm in order to live in peace and harmony with God only? What a wonderful thought to bring the Mind of Christ into our everyday experience instead of duality of good and evil. God only is in control of who is appointed to be the President of the United States of America. God never created evil, but does let us have both good and evil until we come to our senses and believing in who and what we are in God.

November 9-THE EVERGREEN TREE IS WHAT I AM.
Our lives are compared our lives with the Evergreen Tree.
An Evergreen Tree is never affected by winter, summer,
spring or fall or change in the weather. The Evergreen Tree
is always green with chlorophyll. The Tree of Life does
not have disease (losing its peace), sickness, pain or
suffering. The seed of Christ is planted inside of us. It is
learning that death or negative thinking cannot come to a
Spirit Body. Fear thoughts, pain thoughts, and grief
thoughts cause us to have old age. Every cell of our bodies
is being resurrected into perfection of the Spirit Being that
we are.

November 10-WE DO NOT INHERIT HUMAN TRAITS
FROM OUR ANCESTORS? We only inherit the thoughts
of anger, jealousy, disease, addictions, and all things related
to suggestion. We must put a stop to belief that what our
parents had will affect me only if I let the suggestion rule
my life. We go to doctor and he says we have some disease
or affliction, and we believe in his word. Mesmerized and
hypnotic suggestions must stop with me before they began
to rule our lives. Jesus the Christ was tempted in every area
as we are. He did not give in to any temptations because
He knew that they were not true. We must stop listening to
the world human mind that fills us with lies and deceit.

November 11-MY SEARCH IS TO KNOW GOD AND
BE LIKE GOD. I want to be God like in everything I do
and say. I AM a daughter of God with health; happiness;
prosperity; and all good to come to me. The debris in my
mind of anger, hate, no forgiveness, pain and suffering hide
from me God thoughts. Past memories, I can only
remember the great ones and leave the others forgiven. We
only live in the now. I must live each moment with love to
give to everyone I meet. We are all parts of God with a
different plan and purpose like the human body that is one
body with different parts and different plans.

129

November 12-OUR LIVES ARE COMPARED TO A PENCIL THAT IS ALWAYS SHARPENED. A pencil must be sharpened to be able to build our house on the rock of Christ We are building our spiritual house not made with human hands. When I share with you what God shows me, it is not teaching you, but bringing confirmation to you of spiritual truth. We are a family of God. Our human mental pencil will always be dull until we put on the Mind of Christ. The pencil is to write upward in the Spirit realm to the sharpest point. On the pinnacle or highest place within, we can overcome any negative situation or cares of the world to let then disappear. Our Mind is stayed on Christ instead of people behaving ungodly.

November 13-ANIMALS COMPARED TO HUMAN THINKING. The raccoon has a mask that hides his true Identity as a Spirit Beings This raccoon will fight you if you think differently from it. A squirrel digs up our plants and plants human seeds of hate, jealousy and seeds of self instead of Christ. Rabbits hop from one human food to another, but carrots help his eyesight to see in the Spirit realm. The three little pigs must build their house on God within in order for the wolf of the ego thoughts will blow their house down if not built on Christ. The eagle has perfect eye sight to see in the Spirit realm. The eagle only eats live food and not dead doctrines and beliefs of carnal human mind thinking.

November 14-I DON'T CHOOSE TO GOSSIP.
I must not gossip or spread anything I hear about another person. I do not want to add fuel to any fire, but to use water of the River of Life flowing out from me to put out the trash of gossip. I do not want to drink out of the poisoned well of gossip that causes others to hurt. Jesus the Christ said, "Father forgive them because they do not know what they are doing." "Life and death are in the power of the tongue." Words may cause a person's reputation to die with the power of the tongue. We can use non-stick oil like Pam to slide off of us what people do or say.

November 15-MY GARDEN IS FILLED WITH SEEDS OF LOVE. Gal. 6:7-"Whatsoever that a man sows, that shall he also reap." The weeds that crowds out my Godly thoughts of Love, Peace, Joy and Happiness, I must get rid of. The weeds are that I AM not good enough, pretty enough, smart enough are cleaned away. I must dig up judgment and criticism. I can turn over negative, dark thoughts. I can have God thoughts only. Jesus said, "I AM the Vine and you are the branches that produce much fruit and that your fruit may be lasting."

November 16-WE SOLD OUR BIRTHRIGHTS. We were
Spirit Beings, and we sold our birth rights for experiencing
carnal human thoughts and human behavior to satisfy self
and have a world of mortality instead of immortality to
live forever. We fell into the realm of sin which is missing
the mark of Being Christ like, sickness, pain and suffering
and death. We try all kinds of addictions to get that feeling
of magnificent bliss that we had before. God just lets us
have our own free will until we have a need to go back to
God like the Prodigal son. "Even the servants in my
Father's house are treated better than I AM now being
treated." God is just waiting for us to come back to the
Spirit realm where we came from. He welcomes us with
open arms and says, "I was lost, but now I AM found and
this is my beloved son whom I AM proud of."

November 17-WHAT DOES IT MEAN TO BE A
SERVANT? The word servant means to minister; the
elemental forces of Being ever at hand to carry out one's
demands. In the thinking, the Prodigal Son he said my
Father's servants have more than what I have now. Your
feet, legs, arms, heart, lungs and so forth are servants to
your body. Martha in the Bible did much serving. The
doctors and any professionals are servants to us to help us
when we have a need. Jesus the Christ said to be servants to
each other.

November 18-WHAT IS THE VALUE OF EATING
SALMON? Salmon is born in fresh water. We are Spirit
Beings born in the Living Waters of the Spirit Realm.
Salmon lives in salt water most of its life. We live in salt
waters in the human carnal mind in thinking. We get too
much salt of human behavior that causes us to have all
kinds of health problems by believing the lies of the ego
thoughts. Salmon goes up stream like we must go
upstream in the Spirit realm in order to spawn or plant
seeds of inspiration to others. Salmon supports healthy
vision; improves the skin; stabilizes blood pressure;
strengthens memory; helps maintain healthy weight; lowers
cholesterol; lowers cancer risk and many more benefits yet
to receive.

November 19-CAN I TOUCH THE HEM OF GOD'S
GARMENT? A garment is an outer covering of our
bodies. We have a covering of pure Light underneath this
physical body which radiates outward by our aura. Jesus
rent the veil that was hiding our Spirit Body to make us
aware that we are Spirit beings with a body of immortality.
Even the hem of the garment of Christ is very powerful to
touch. It will be healing to the body because of the virtue
coming out of the Christ's body. Virtue means moral
excellence; good quality; moral one; chastity-pure Spirit.
This garment is seamless having no human hands to cause
us to believe that we have a physical body and live in a
physical universe.

November 20-I EAT ONLY THE PURE NECTAR OF THE SPIRIT REALM. 2 Corinthians 2:15-"We are a sweet fragrance of Christ aroma from life to life." God gave us Bees. What could be sweeter than honey? Honey, Bee Pollen and Royal Jelly are complete foods. They are so pure that man cannot duplicate them with man -made knowledge. The word Deborah means a Bee who was a woman judge over all of Israel (means Prince with God) The bee goes to the flowers of pure nectar (Truth). Each bee has a separate special plan and purpose to have the sweet honey to give to us.

November 21-WHAT DOES I AM MEAN? Everything that follows I AM, we have. I AM health, I AM free of pain. I AM Love, Peace, Joy, Happiness and have all the attributes of God. I AM debt free, I AM abundance, I AM God's Masterpiece. I AM a diamond in the rough. "I AM crucified with Christ and I AM also resurrected with Christ." Crucified means death to the old Adam human, carnal nature and man-made rules. Resurrection means I AM a New Person in Christ, and I have only God thoughts.

November 22-WE HAVE TO DIVORCE THE OLD LAW. The Spirit part of us is God. The soul part of us is the individual expression of the Living God. The soul part of us fell into my way, my individual thinking, Edging God Out, I can do it my way without God. We became a Living Soul instead of a Life given Spirit. Now when we realize that the Spirit and the Soul is married as one, we magnify God and know the words of Truth spoken to us. The bride has made herself ready for the marriage that is created by God for eternity. We are all bid to come to the Marriage Feast of the Lamb. So now, we must be divorced from the law of sin, missing the mark of Being, sickness, pain, suffering and death to know a higher law of Love and eternal life.

November 23-ARE YOU PREGNANT WITH THE SEED OF CHRIST? When you are pregnant, you have a lot of time for preparation. You have back pains, leg pains, swelling, gaining weight. David was 17 when he was anointed by the prophet Samuel to become King. He had to be nice to Saul who was trying to kill the Christ in him. The first King was the ego thoughts and the world of human thinking and human beliefs. David was 30 which is the number of starting to minister into completion of plan and purpose and a cycle of renewal when he became King

November 24-HARMONY HAS TO BE CHOSEN IN OUR LIVES. Agreement in ideas, actions; pleasing combination on musical tones is the meaning of Harmony. I want to be in agreement and in One Accord with God. My walk with God is in control of the path I AM to follow. Light means understanding and causes darkness to go away. Darkness was never there when the light is on. I let go of human thoughts and illusions that I have created with my own mind of being instead of God. I can feel the Unconditional Love of God in everything I do and say. I can recharge my human (lowest of human dirt thinking) battery that has any negative unbalanced situation to the Light and Harmony. The purple flame of Royalty shines bright in my Spiritual Being.

November 25-WE CAN STEP INTO THE UNKOWN. God tells us something to move further into the Spirit Realm, but does not give you any details of the future. God gives us step by step instructions when we need to know the direction to follow. If we did not take the first step to the unknown, we may miss the best for our lives for the now. The human mind says that is impossible, but God is the God of the impossible. When we follow the first step, we can walk on water and fly with wings of an eagle to go high in the Spirit Realm. We take faith to believe the unknown without any questions from reasoning of the carnal human mind.

NOVEMBER 26-FALSE ALARMS IS SOMETHING THAT IS NOT REAL. The carnal human mind gives us false alarms that we panic and think they are real. Negative thoughts are false alarms because they are not true. Gossip is a false alarm that ruins a person's reputation, and that is not true. Love is a healing balm that touches us from head to toe. Anger is a false alarm of fear-"Perfect Love cast out fear." Pain is the false alarm because there is no pain in God. I AM a perfect Spirit Being and my Identity cannot be stolen by a thought. I can see people as sandpaper causing my Pearl to be round and smooth.

November 27-LET US PEEL OFF THE ONION SKINS STEP BY STEP. The outer layer of the skin is our physical self that is led by the carnal mind in thinking. We peel this layer of the onion to have the body of Spirit that is our Real Self underneath the physical body to the body of immortality. The next layer of skin is to peel off the thought that our real self is controlled by the carnal mind of sin-missing the mark of Being God Like, pain, suffering, and death is our only reality. The legs, arms and everything in the body can be controlled by the human mind OR the Mind of Christ to be able to function.

November 28-LITTLE THINGS ARE IMPORTANT TO BE THANKFUL FOR. Thanking God for being able to see because somebody can't see at all. Thanks for a family, friends, homes, cars, jobs, weather hot or cold. "Thank God in everything no matter what the circumstances may be The lessons are to not choose good and evil again. Know that in every situation that everything will be alright. When we change our perception, things will change. We can think We can think different about circumstances and people. Nothing can be impossible in life because, we have a God of Impossibility. Just when you think you will stay in the cocoon forever and never see the light of day, that is when you become a beautiful butterfly

November 29-I AM GOD'S MASTERPIECE. Masterpiece means something made or done with expert skill. You are one of a kind and can only fit in the one piece of the giant puzzle. There will never be another like you. Your fingerprints are not like any other. Stop speaking wrong of yourself. I AM a different person and can talk to anyone We have been painted by the most famous of all painters, God. Did you know that People see you as you see yourself? See yourself as a Child and Family of God, beautiful, strong, talented and very valuable. You are Royalty, thinking like Royalty, talking like Royalty, walking and acting like Royalty. You are excellent in every way. .

November 30-YOUR LIFE MAKES A DIFFERENCE. You are important to God. God is in each of us exactly the same whether we know it or not. God fragmented Him. God is ALL IN ALL and not All in One. You soul is the individual personality or your Identity as a Spirit Being. Your light dispels darkness. Do you have any idea what affect you have on other people? You may never know how you have changed someone life by a word of Love and Power. You have a special plan and purpose that affects the whole just like the human body parts each unique and cannot do without the others Never doubt your importance by listening to negative thoughts of your own mind.

DECEMBER

December 1-WE NEED PEOPLE AND SITUATIONS IN OUR LIVES. People and situations are needed. Nothing happens by accident or by chance but by Divine order Everyone in your life is either to teach them something or for you to learn something from them. Our goal in life is to help someone feel better about them to learn who and what they are. We have erasers on pencils to correct our mistakes. "Be you transformed by the renewing of your mind."

December 2-HAVE YOU LOST YOUR WAY?
Did you forget who and what you are? Did you ever go in a parking lot and forget where you parked the car? This is what happened to us when we went into another dimension instead of a Spirit Being. We forgot where our true home was and began to roam around without a purpose and make everything Instead of God. We do have someone who came to show us our way back home in a Loving Home of peace and Love. The man Jesus came in the flesh and taught us about the Christ of our Being.

December 3-WHY ARE YOU STILL IN YOUR MOTHER'S WOMB? When a person is pregnant they usually have lots of aches and pains. They can hardly wait for the child to be born. We can't stay in our Mother's womb forever. We are born again in the Spirit realm. In the realm of carnal thinking we have sin which is missing the mark of Being God like, sickness, pain, suffering and even death to the Spirit realm. We try to do everything by our self and satisfy the desires of flesh. We must go from the worm state of eating the dirt of human thinking to the cocoon state to separate all the thoughts of human thinking to the thoughts of God only to come out as a beautiful butterfly eating only the pure nectar of the Spirit realm of God only.

December 4-DO YOU WANT TO KEEP ON JUDGING OTHERS? "Judge not, that you be not judged." For with what judgment you judge, you shall be judged." This means whatever you give out to others; it will come back to you. It is called the "Law of Attraction." Let us give Love, Peace, Joy and Happiness. I AM not giving out hate, ungodliness, jealousy or any human carnal thinking to others, it is a law. It is just like a ball that is thrown up, must come down. This is the law of CAUSE AND EFFECT. When we accept others just the way they are, we recognize their own uniqueness, beauty, and the puzzle piece that can only fit in one place.

December 5-ARE YOU RIDING IN A LEAKY BOAT? A boat is something we ride in. When we have a leaky boat, it sinks. A boat that is filled with Love, Peace, Joy, and Happiness sails along and receive new enthusiasm each day. A boat that has negative human thoughts and emotions like fear (false evidence appearing real) jealousy, enviousness, false beliefs, and anything that is not Godlike is going to sink little by little. Jesus is like the ferry boat that carries us across the fierce weather of human life with its ups and downs when we can't seem to find our way back to God where we came from.

December 6-DO YOU EVER FAIL TO READ DIRECTIONS? Do you try to put something together and fail to read the directions finding you are doing it over again because there is one part left out? The ego thoughts that Edge God Out always wants to do things its own way instead of following the pattern of the directions of God. We think we are justified in our thinking to hurt others. God is knocking at our door and wanting to come in. When we let God in, God takes us into another dimension. We let God knock and knock and say I have plenty of time to receive God only. I know it all and I AM satisfied to stay where I AM and I know it all.

December 7-WE CAN TEACH ABOUT GOD WITH DEEP REVELATIONS. The best way to teach anyone about God is to be a great example. We cannot preach to others, but just BE. We know that we are children of God. We can change our world by thinking differently. We take the responsibility of our own decisions knowing that God forgives me so I can't blame another for my actions. We can reflect God's love, truth, and unity. We can offer a helping hand to those in darkness by shining our light of understanding. I AM a channel of Love, peace and light to all that I meet. I AM so thankful that God writes my lessons through me to spread the word.

141

December 8-DO YOU HAVE A LOT OF UNWANTED EMOTIONS? Have you decided to forgive a person and when you see that person, you have those same emotions of feeling hurt, unhappy, disturbed and critical? Sit down, and start thinking about all the good and beauty you see in that person. Have a quiet time with God remembering all you have to be thankful for and seeing that person as a Child of God that "Forgive them Father, they know not what they are doing." When I AM feeling pain, proclaim I have Perfect Health, Abundance, Love, Peace, Joy and Happiness.

December 9-WHEN WAS YOUR BIRTH? Your real self was not birthed from your earthly father and mother Adam and Eve represent all of mankind not just two people. Our fall was when we forgot that our birth was Divine, Immortality, and Spirit Beings. Adam and Eve birthed mortal human beings. In Adam, we all die, but in Christ we all are birthed into Life. How can I re-member who and what I AM unless the pattern of God is here on earth. Could I BE one of the lost sheep who forgot to follow the Shepherd and decided to go my OWN WAY?

December 10 I AM IN HARMONY WITH GOD TODAY. You may feel isolated from others from time to time. In time of trouble, you find out that many people are there for you that do not keep in contact with you to show their Love for you on a daily basis. Today, I desire to be One with God. No more separate thoughts, words, actions from ego thoughts. I can feel a reconciliation (make friendly again; settle a quarrel) taking place deep inside of me. I can no longer put my attention to human carnal thoughts. Do you Love Yourself? Let us go higher in dimension where there is no pain, sin, suffering and death. My body is healthy and free of pain.

December 11-MIRACLES CAN HAPPEN FOR TODAY. Miracles are a gift of God. A miracle is when a child is conceived and is born! It is a miracle when a worm (lowest of human thinking that eats everything) is transformed into a cocoon (time to choose the Best Truth and to glean only the Words of God and not the ego thoughts that EDGE GOD OUT. The real meaning of miracles is a shift in our perception from the ego's world of sin, sickness, death, fear, feeling of less than to the Holy Spirit's world of Unconditional Love, Peace, Joy and Happiness. It is a miracle to KNOW that God is in me and Loves me and you exactly the same. It is a Miracle when one's unbelieving thoughts are turned to truths. EXPECT A MIRACLE!

December 12-ARE YOU GETTING FREE FROM HUMAN THINKING? Gal. 5:1--"Stand fast in the liberty wherewith Christ (anointed ones) has made us free." We can be at peace in the midst of chaos (complete disorder). "We are the children of God and have the Spirit of Christ within us." I can celebrate the Gift of Life. God is within us at all times. The Truth sets me free from my worries, anxiety, fear (false evidence appearing real), and any false thoughts that I may have at this moment. "He healed all that was sick." I AM the Lord that heals thee."

December 13-DO WE OVERCOME DEATH? "We rise up above death by letting LIFE express to its absolute fullness." The scripture speaks of dead as not remembering who and what they are as Spirit Beings and Unconscious of the Truth and being asleep. We die to sin (archery term meaning missing the mark of Being God like), sickness, carnal thinking, and be alive to Righteousness, Peace, Love and Happiness. You have died with Christ to material ways of looking at things and escaped from crude and elemental notions and teachings of external existence. You have been raised with Christ sharing His resurrection from the dead and now seeking the eternal treasure of Christ.

December 14-I AM NOT ALONE. "God never leaves us or forsakes us." "God's grace is sufficient in everything that God would have me and you to do." The everlasting arms bear us up in the Truth that sustains us and sets us free from all thoughts that EDGE GOD OUT. When we let our words partake of God's nature, we can ask and it shall be done. We must let Go and Let God. I can make false appearances of stress, unbelief, fear and any thoughts that are not God transformed into precious words of truth. "Knowing that all things work together for Good and only Thoughts of Victory remain."

December 15-A MAGNET THAT DOES ATTRACTS GOD. A magnet is something that attracts. The Law of Attraction is what we give out comes back to us. We have the seed of Christ planted in us in conception of creation. The tares (weeds of human thinking) grow at the same time as the wheat (spiritual qualities). We want to attract Love, Peace, Joy and Happiness in our lives. God burns out our fear, stress thoughts to Love thoughts. In the "Toy Story," Buss Light-year tried to be an astronaut, but he was just a toy. Seeds do not grow in soil of carnal human thinking. Our consciousness is raised into another dimension when we "ARE" instead of trying to become.

December 16-MIRACLES ARE LIKE LOOKING IN A MIRROR THAT REFLECTS LOVE. When we have negative thoughts about any subject, if we nip the thoughts in the bud, we don't have to carry the thoughts out to be creative in our lives. You are like Snow White. You must look in the mirror and see that YOU ARE THE FAIREST of all the thoughts that destroy. The wicked witch of our ego thoughts thinks that she is on the throne and is in control of our thinking. But, Snow White you are the fairest very expression of God on this earth of them all.

December 17- GOD IS CHANGELESS. "Be still, and know THAT, I AM GOD, I change not." The signs of "Stop, Look and Listen' stopped many accidents by a railroad track. We can put up a sign in our thinking saying stop worry, confusion, fear (false evidence appearing real), anxiety, stress and any other emotion or action that is not God like. The only thing we change is our negative thinking that EDGES GOD OUT. We cannot be deceived with negative ideas that flow through our minds. Nothing can distort the beauty of God but our own perception of what God is.

December 18-CAN YOU PRAY FOR THE IMPOSSIBLE? Two blind men cried out to Jesus. "Have mercy on us to be able to see." Jesus knew they were blind, but they asked for the impossible and believed it would happen. Sometimes it seems that what you ask God for will never come to pass. These desires may not be for your best interest. We should always ask for God's will to be done. Is it for the best of your Being? God is not in pain and suffering. You have all the characteristic of the Living God. That includes Unconditional Love, Joy and Happiness NOW.

December 19-ARE YOU CONTROLING YOUR TONGUE? "Life and death are in the tongue." You can really hurt a person's life forever with evil speaking of that person. I want to speak only the Truths of God to every person I meet and call them a Holy Encounter. "The words of sticks and stones may hurt my bones, but words will not hurt me." This is not true because words are deep wounds that cannot be healed sometimes. Sometimes we say things that do not have the meaning that people take. Stop before we speak and ask the Holy Spirit what to say at all times to lift a person up and never bring them down.

145

December 20-YOU CAN OVERCOME EVIL WITH GOOD. All the seemingly bad things in our past are turned to learning lessons not to ever choose again? Joseph in the bible was sold by his brothers, but he chose to let them be free and forgive them by saying, "You meant it for evil, but God meant it for good." We are to keep our eyes single on the Spirit within us, which is eternal and embraces all that is good. Whatever law we give out, we attract. If we are mean to others, we will attract meanness. Every person in our lives is there for a reason. So experience is needed for us to grow spiritually and to remember we have a choice to attract what we want in our lives by the LAW OF ATTRACTION.

December 21-I WANT THE WISDOM OF GOD. "For the Lord gives us Wisdom: out of His mouth cometh knowledge and understanding." Proverbs 2:6. King Solomon asked for Wisdom. He was greater in wisdom than all the kings of the earth. The word Solomon means whole, entire, complete, and peace. Solomon was the third king of Israel and choose peace instead of war. We are the tabernacle of the Living God. The body build by man is transfigured to an eternal body not made with human hands. Solomon was the king who could build the temple of God with Love and Peace. Solomon represents the body changed to the body of Christ that had no limits and much potential. This body can go into another dimension and walk through walls and appear to anyone with just a thought when we learn how.

December 22-NOW IS THE TIME TO BE BORN AGAIN.
Colossians 3:10-"And have put on the new man, which is
renewed in knowledge after the image of him that created
him." We must be born again from above, and we do not
go back in our mother's womb of this world of carnal
thinking. This new birth makes us to remember that we are
a child of God with all the aspects of royalty. The old has
passed away and all things become new. We can co-create
with God if we only can have new thoughts and ideas and
plunge into the River of Life flowing out from me that
makes the lame to walk and the blind to see. Positive
speaking becomes more important..

December 23-I CAN CO-CREATE WITH GOD. "And I
say unto you, ask, and it shall be given you, seek and you
shall find, knock and it shall be opened to you." Luke
11:9. When the door is open, we must go in. The
Kingdom of God is within. I can build a better world and
clear my thoughts of negativity, feelings and attitudes. Just
like a skein of thread with many colors has an infinite
potential to create beautiful masterpieces, God can change
our lives to follow the pattern in the heavens instead of
human thinking and human ways. God wants to give us
everything that God has.

December 24-TODAY IS A DAY OF GOD'S LOVE. Did you know that Love is a Law? When you give out Love, it comes back to you as Love. Loving one another is the reason why we have harmony and peace. Love gives appreciation to other for what they are and what they do. I can give Love to everyone I meet today. Love is an essence felt from one person to another. Love is a feeling you receive when you know that Love is given to you. God is Love. So we are Love, also. "The law is, "Love God and Love your neighbor as yourself." It is very important to know who you are, and to Love your real self which is the child of God. Love is a healing balm to put in the wounds of pain, suffering, sickness, sin, and death.

December 25-WHAT IS THE MEANING OF CHRISTMAS? Christmas is the birth of Jesus the Christ, used as a symbol for rebirth of Christ in me. The Christmas story tells about a babe that does not grow. Christmas is the time of year where families gather together to renew their love for each other. Everything in the Christmas story is about the story of Christ realized in us. Today we celebrate the incarnation of the Spirit with us. "The same spirit that raised Christ from the dead dwells within me. It will quicken my mortal body that Spirit that dwells in me." The whole story of the birth of Christ to every detail is about the Christ born in us.

December 26-GOD SEES ME AS A TREASURE. I see myself beautiful, godly, whole, and complete. I see no guilt in me. within me. I open myself to continual renewal, living in gratitude, joy and wisdom. I see myself as royalty and a child of God. I AM a perfect creation. I have all the attributes of God. I AM unique. There is not another like me. I AM one of a kind. I AM a unique manifestation of the Living God to those who do not know God. Without me God is not complete to be in each of us.

December 27-HEAVEN IS WITHIN ME. "Now we have received, not the spirit of the world, but the spirit which is of God; that we might know the things that are freely given to us of God." 1st Corinthians 2:12 Did you know that heaven is not a place, but a condition in your own mind? We can have heaven on earth, if we choose beauty, health, happiness and most of all love. The Love of God can change all my thoughts and all my problems if I will let it. Change our thinking and make this world heaven instead of hell.

December 28-LIFE IS BETTER EACH DAY. We have eternal life. When the body dies it goes into one dimension into another. This is not the final phase. Life will keep on going and growing forever. I open myself up to receive more life each day and get rid of doom and gloom and negative thinking. I must fulfill my plan and purpose here. We go from one garment to another garment. Life is a flow and if life is not a flow, we are not happy. I AM an eternal being to experience life forever. I can fully live fully with God in every thought and breath of my life. Without God in my life, I AM nothing.

December 29-YOU ARE A REFLECTION OF GOD. When you look in the water, the water shows a reflection of you as if it was you. God created us in the image of God after the pattern in the heavens. You can look in a mirror and see your reflection as you. Mirror, mirror on the wall, who is the fairest of them all? It is you Snow White; you are the fairest of them all. If you could only see the beautiful person you are with many talents and all the attributes of God, you would never say anything about yourself again that is negative. You would know that you are very unique with not another to be like you.

December 30-I HAVE THE MARK OF GOD ON MY FOREHEAD. My thoughts only are the thoughts of God. My mind is stamped with all that is good. I will step out of the tomb of not knowing and understanding the things of God. The mark of the beast is totally man's mind, will and emotions. I can't think carnal thoughts of manmade religions, rituals and teachings if I have the Mark of God on my mind. I can only be an individual creation of God.

December 31-THIS IS THE END OF MY YEAR'S
ANGEL MESSENGERS TO YOU.

These angel messengers were a pleasure to write to
you with much time taken with much care. I hope
to have enlightened you to the truth of God in a
deeper way. The learning about God will never
end. Each day we will receive much more wisdom
than the day before. Remember the word I AM is
very powerful. I AM Love, peace, joy and
Happiness. Your words are very powerful, so be
very careful what you say. Let the words of your
mouth bring peace and comfort to another person.

Made in the USA
Columbia, SC
27 August 2021